Good Little GREEK GIRL

A Story of Manipulation, Control and Abuse That Crossed the Cultural Divide

Dama Koupa

First published by Ultimate World Publishing 2025
Copyright © 2025 Dama Koupa

ISBN

Paperback: 978-1-923583-14-6
Ebook: 978-1-923583-17-7

Dama Koupa has asserted her rights under the Copyright, Designs and Patents Act 1988 to be identified as the author of this work. The information in this book is based on the author's experiences and opinions. The publisher specifically disclaims responsibility for any adverse consequences which may result from use of the information contained herein. Permission to use information has been sought by the author. Any breaches will be rectified in further editions of the book.

All rights reserved. No part of this publication may be reproduced, stored in or introduced into a retrieval system, or transmitted in any form, or by any means (electronic, mechanical, photocopying, recording or otherwise) without the prior written permission of the author. Any person who does any unauthorised act in relation to this publication may be liable to criminal prosecution and civil claims for damages. Enquiries should be made through the publisher.

Cover design: Ultimate World Publishing
Layout and typesetting: Ultimate World Publishing
Editor: Alex Floyd-Douglass

Ultimate World Publishing
Diamond Creek,
Victoria Australia 3089
www.writeabook.com.au

For my daughter.

Live your life with integrity, bravery and strength.

Dama Koupa is a subsidiary of

Contents

Preface	1
Chapter 1: Be a Good Girl	7
Chapter 2: To Be Worthy	13
Chapter 3: The Wedding March vs `Jaws´ Theme Music	23
Chapter 4: My Own `Big Fat Greek Wedding´	27
Chapter 5: Fuck You and Yo´ Mamma!	31
Chapter 6: The Aftermath	39
Chapter 7: Racist to the Core	45
Chapter 8: Great Grandmother's Curse	51
Chapter 9: Umm… That's Not Normal	57
Chapter 10: Just Like the Movies	71
Chapter 11: I'm So Tired, But That Never Stopped Me	75
Chapter 12: A Narc of My Own	85
Chapter 13: Discovering and Embodying My Life Path	95
Chapter 14: Quotes That Felt Personal	105
Chapter 15: Nothing Changes, If Nothing Changes!	111
Chapter 16: Goosfraba	115

Chapter 17: The Cut Off Game   121

Chapter 18: Understanding Beyond the Physical   129

Chapter 19: The Way the Cycle Repeats Itself   135

Chapter 20: Speak Up   139

Chapter 21: Dear Mum   143

Chapter 22: Dear Dad   147

Chapter 23: It's Not the End   151

Resources   153

About the Author   157

Preface

GOOD LITTLE GREEK GIRL

Welcome. This book is a record of life as I have lived it, to the best of my recollection. I do not care if others remember it in a different way. That is their story and this is mine. Everyone is entitled to their own perspective and their perspective is none of my business. Nor is their opinion of me.

My real name is *not* Dama Koupa. This nickname means so much to me as it was given to me by my grandmother, who was also shared the same name. She protected me when I was a child and continued to protect me since her passing in 1997, through my dreams and psychic mediums.

This book is dedicated to her.

We shared the same wit and sense of humour and a sharp tongue because we are both so brutally honest. She would have wanted me to be brave and honest. I believe if she were still alive, she would have had my back in both of my miserable marriages. She would have spoken up when no one else did. Instead, I was alone to fight my battles. My marriages may have been saved if she was still here. She would have put them in their place. She wouldn't have let them get away with anything.

I am the daughter of Greek Immigrants. The first generation born in Australia. I struggled living two lives and feeling completely lost not fitting into either. If you can relate – this book is for you.

You do not have to be Greek. Perhaps you just have parents like mine – stuck in the ways of their childhood and forcing their beliefs, morals, racism, hatred and traditions on to

PREFACE

you, hating if you ever thought for yourself – declaring it disrespectful if you ever challenged them.

You were never a bad person, but you never felt like you were 'good enough'. Trying to find a balance between being a good kid and a capable, independent adult.

Do you ever feel like you have to wear different masks, around different people? Do you act differently depending on who is watching or listening, or monitoring?

Do you ever feel so out of touch, not knowing which of your personalities is the real you?

It took me 42 years to realise I am not my parents' story. Nor am I anyone else's.

I am writing this, hoping that someone that has walked a mile in my shoes can see that they are not alone and there is a chance for real change.

You must be willing to sacrifice the old you, burn a few bridges and get on with a new life.

Not everyone will understand your journey, but who cares? They never understood your past either if we're being honest. So, why would we care if they did not get it now? You do not owe anyone explanations.

I have taken everything I have learnt over the last 40 years and incorporated as much as I could for you into this book.

GOOD LITTLE GREEK GIRL

I encourage you to look these people up and see where your experience takes you.

No two journeys are the same.

I was always called the 'school lawyer'. I was friends with everyone – especially if you were the odd one out and getting picked on or looked down on by others. I was always happy to get to know people and not take other's opinions of people seriously. I always hated gossip. That was probably because I hated the gossip that would circulate the Greek grapevine.

I hated it because everyone gossiped about everyone. They were all hypocrites. Some exaggerators and liars. Gossip controlled my entire family. The thought of being gossiped about kept everyone on eggshells. Because the gossipers did not want to be gossiped about. How exhausting.

Everyone I knew was worried about what would be said about them so of course the only solution was to be perfect all the time.

Go to church. Be seen always looking well-dressed, well-behaved, well-spoken. Code for: do not scratch, people with think you have nits. Do not yell, people will think you have a bad temper. Do not interrupt, people will think you have bad manners.

I always stood up for everyone. Slowly, I started to shut up. After years of being told to shut up and mind my own business. I was told I did not understand what was going on. I was told that I was too emotional, and my opinion was automatically ignored.

PREFACE

Just a girl that knew nothing. Nothing was my business, even if it was *me* they were discussing as if I were not in the room.

I wanted to write this book for all the other children of Immigrants' children that may be in the same boat. The earlier generations came to Australia and are desperate to maintain their identity, to a fault.

They do the best they can as parents, but they themselves have not found who they are without the identity bestowed upon them. Their identities were forged by the generations before them. The world has changed but their childhood trauma still dictates their life, and they still succumb to the controls of the past.

The impact of the next generations stuck in limbo between the two realities, wearing the good girl *mask* in front of strangers because of fear of rejection and judgment. The sad part is when we wear the masks in front of the people that are meant to support us and love us unconditionally. My generation were scared to open up and communicate with our own parents. It was a survival instinct.

I recognise the patterns and I do not want my daughter to be the next generation trapped in this loop of ultimate grief.

Everything I've fought for so far, is so that the future generations can live more authentic, happy, peaceful lives.

I would rather be the black sheep now so future generations can be free. The trauma we don't fix, we pass on to the next generation.

GOOD LITTLE GREEK GIRL

We are not alone. We are not *bad* for not conforming. We are 100% perfect the way we are and we are not responsible for *everyone else's* happiness.

We are not the story that our parents told us, nor are they the story their parents told them.

We are our own people.

We own our own destiny.

Our own journey.

We should each allow ourselves to find our own truth, ultimately finding our soul's purpose and only that will bring us the peace we crave.

There is such a thing as a *new normal* and we just need to allow ourselves to have it.

Chapter 1

Be a Good Girl

GOOD LITTLE GREEK GIRL

A phrase that still creeps me out.

"Be a good girl."

My first memory I have is holding a blanket over my head, my eyes shut tight, and my face scrunched up. I was trying to stay totally still and quiet while an older relative was touching me in a way that relatives should never touch. I had no idea what was happening. I knew it felt nice and tickly. I am human and physical touch is a physiological pleasure.

I had a feeling it was wrong because the boys were always so secretive about luring me upstairs and getting us to hide under the blanket. I knew no one was allowed to touch me there but they told me it was okay because we were family, and it was going to feel nice if I let them. They told me it was okay because we all bathed together, so what was the difference? We are always all naked together. Nothing new. They had already seen my private parts and I had seen theirs. So what?

They told me they did this stuff with girls at school all the time. It didn't matter because we were all kids and its only adults that aren't meant to touch children.

"Don't be so frigid."

I didn't know what that meant but I knew it was an insult. It was somehow a threat to my place in the tribe.

I was so young, not yet in my double digits' era and very innocent. My much older relative, however, was given access to pornography and encouraged to explore and enjoy his sexuality. I'm sure his parents never thought that he would do these things to his own relatives but there was no attempt to make it stop when they found out what was happening.

It was up to me to fight him off and say no. But it was also my responsibility to keep the peace and keep everyone happy because I didn't want to be the one that was causing a fight. I didn't want to be the troublemaker. I didn't want to be hated if I said no. These people were my entire circle, and I was with them every day.

What would happen to me if they all hated me?

All the adults in my family were fully aware of the situation, yet they all seemed happy enough to keep the daily routine exactly the same. They dropped us off and went to work. Good luck kiddo.

"Be good."

What did 'good' even mean? Don't fight, don't upset your grandparents, help with cleaning and cooking, don't lie, don't make too much noise, don't disturb the adults – especially if we have guests. Be seen if you have to but never heard. Hug and kiss every adult, no matter how uncomfortable you are. Look your best so people can praise how well your parents have dressed you well, but don't ever think of praising yourself – that's vanity. Vanity is a sin.

The only one that tried to help me was my grandmother. She was the one that would check on me to see if I was ok during the day. She was the one that tried to keep us busy where she could see us. There were seven of us under her care. It was a huge task. She was the one that told the parents what was happening.

The boys were never shamed or punished for what they were doing. But I was. I was told not to *let* it happen anymore. I was made to explain why I *let* it happen in the first place and recall in detail how it happened and what had happened.

My mum threatened, *"Tell me everything you did, or I'll tell your father."*

I knew that meant more punishment. Dad was the one that smacked. So, I told her what happened, hoping for a hug or some protection. If I was in my parents' shoes, I'd be asking what happened so I could confront the child and his parents to put a proper stop to it. But their priorities were different. I got neither the hug or the protection...

Instead, I just kept getting sent back over and over to spend time with the same people.

Now in my 40s and finally brave enough to talk about it, I found that I was not his only victim. I wish I knew how to tell someone without judgment. I wish I could have stood up for myself without getting in trouble for it.

I was conditioned to keep my mouth shut.

It was so hard for me to tell. I thought that perhaps he was going to get in trouble. I thought then I would be in trouble for getting them in trouble. But I took the risk because I thought maybe they would help protect me and help make it stop.

I quickly realised that I was the one getting in trouble, even though I was the vulnerable one being targeted.

It would always start the same.

"Let's play Tiggy. Let's play 40 all home. Let's play and kiss. Let's play stuck in the mud."

And then the dread hit every time I'd hear, *"Let's play Mums and Dads or kings and queens."*

Then the rules, *"Mums and Dads kiss and have sex. Pretend I just got home from work, and we're supposed to have sex!"*

Although I was never penetrated in the conventional sense, my heart and soul were penetrated and filled with guilt, shame and hatred. I was passed around the males of the family once the ringleader told them what I had let him do, they wanted to try, too.

I only recently understood that I had been groomed.

I fought back one day. It was getting too much. Of course, I got in trouble for screaming and yelling and embarrassing my parents while we were visiting someone's house. But it was worth it.

I didn't care if I got in trouble. I had to protect myself because I was scared this was never going to stop. I spent the night sitting on the floor next to my mother. She kept telling me to go away and play with the other kids. She thought I was interested in the gossip the adults were sharing. No one ever checked why I was there. They just assumed and scalded me for it.

From a super young age, I felt that no one had my back. No one loved me.

Reputation was more important than the truth and justice. I was a tool to please others, and I was to sacrifice, shut up and put up with whatever was thrown at me, and I was just to accept it and keep the peace for everyone else. I always heard, *"What are others going to say?"*

I couldn't imagine this happening to my now eight year old daughter. I will happily kick anyone's ass, who would dare touch my daughter. And I would not give a fuck about what people said or thought of me. I wouldn't think twice about upsetting people. I know my priorities now.

My baby is precious.

Chapter 2

To Be Worthy

GOOD LITTLE GREEK GIRL

Why wasn't I precious to my parents?

Why didn't they love me?

Nobody loved me!

I was just there to be a good girl. Be seen but not heard. A token of my parents' achievements. Wow look, they ticked the right boxes – bought a house, got married, had kids. ✓✓✓

Well done.

Now you must continue to earn ticks, or are you even worthy?

1. Impossibly clean house, not lived in and always ready for visitors to drop in unannounced. ✓
2. Knowing all the gossip about everyone else. ✓
3. Having enough food to feed 10x more people to show you are a good host. ✓
4. Inviting hundreds of people to your child's wedding, despite not seeing them for 20 years. ✓
5. Don't show anyone you have problems at home. ✓
6. Only have a few friends that are approved – usually your own family members, because no one else is as good as the family you are born into. We are superior. ✓
7. If you're a mother/ wife: remember you are inferior to all men and respecting your husband meant being scared of him and doing everything humanly (and superhumanly) possible to uphold his incredibly ridiculous demands. Heaven forbid, you give him something to complain about to his mother! ✓

Don't forget to also have a job and bring money into the house, as well as tend to the children and all of the domestic duties. Don't ever complain or get tired or stressed.

Are you grateful for having a husband? Now keep him happy. Even if he cheats on you multiple times and teaches your kids to lie to you – still respect him and worship the ground he walks on and accept him back when he's good and ready to apologise. If he's ever ready. They may never be ready.

I mean, was it even his fault? He had urges. It's not his fault if someone was sexy and tempted him. It's the 'slut's' fault, not your married husband's fault. Were you even enough for him?

"There must have been a reason he cheated, what did you do?"

Thank for setting me straight, Mum. I always thought it was like the movies – when the women tell their cheating husbands to pack their bags and kick him out of the house. Silly me. Just stay married for as long as possible so people can't talk bad about you. Eww. Imagine being a divorcee – with kids!? No one will ever speak to me again. I'll never find another man to marry me. I'm just someone's *used goods*. Someone's old problem.

Even if I cry every day, never admit that you are worth better.

"Get over yourself, who do you think you are?"

"Just be happy to be married. Don't forget, you have to stay together for the kids."

Show the kids a great example of adult life. That will prepare them for the real world. Be submissive ladies, or there will be fights and they will all be your fault. Hurry home so dinner is on the table for him. Don't let him walk into an empty house. He's going to be worried and obviously have to accuse you of having an affair.

Where else would you have been? Why did you have to put that thought into his mind? You brought this upon yourself for not following the rules. You know he likes you to greet him at home with a hot meal at the end of the day. He can't serve himself, even if the food is ready, sitting on the stove. Don't expect him to know where the crockery and cutlery are. Don't ever expect him to serve himself, and certainly not the kids and never you. That's your job... duh! If not to serve your husband, why did you even get married?

Last but not least: Be careful of what you do, say, wear, because what will other people think and what will they say and what will my reputation be?

Are we getting the picture yet? I feel sick in the guts, talking about this stuff. Reliving that ugly feeling of disappointment, fear, disrespect, worthlessness. Eurgh!

The parents of the abuser told me not to tell my parents. They also told the other victims to do the same. The Golden Child remains protected at all costs.

The definition of the Golden Child:

1. Be a boy.
2. Be the eldest.
3. Be named after your father's father and carry the family name.

My parents did find out about it, and I was in trouble, and I had to be held accountable for my actions. I had to tell a secret I was told to keep. I was confused because I was always taught to shut up and put up to keep the peace, now I was being interrogated and asked to justify why I was letting myself be abused?

When I spoke up, I got the typical, *"No one likes a whinger. No one likes a liar. No one likes troublemakers. What they did is no big deal, but what you let them do is terrible. What did you do to make them do that?"*

Gaslit to the max! I was losing my mind. I felt insane every day. I couldn't understand why my family was so fucked up. Why were they so toxic? Why they were so... them? I hated them! Part of me still does. Not all wounds heal with time.

I already understood that virginity was very important to my future husband. Sex before marriage was a great sin and no one would ever want me if I wasn't a virgin. It was the biggest flex as a potential bride. We had something my girl cousins and I called 'nifi points' translated means, 'worthy to be a wife, points'. Like, were you worthy of being married?

GOOD LITTLE GREEK GIRL

Start 'em young.

If not, then what the hell is wrong with you? You don't love or respect your parents enough to do the right thing and get married and have kids? Don't you know you are worthless unless you are married before 25 and have kids and a mortgage? Are you a slut? Are you lazy? Are you untidy? Are you vain? Do you love yourself?

(queue sarcasm) The audacity!

I tried to be the perfect daughter, niece, cousin granddaughter etc., but resentment was building up. I knew that I would never have the same freedoms that my big brother had. He was allowed to have as many girlfriends as he wanted. He was told that 'Xeni' (non-Greek) girls were 'all sluts' and he could have his fun with them before he was ready to settle down and marry a good little Greek girl.

Sadly, this was very a common attitude among Greek boys. He was allowed to play soccer, but no sport for me. I did ballet, but it didn't last very long. The guilt of being a financial burden on my parents was enough to make me hate the glitter and frills of dance. Plus, it took too much time, and parking was a mess, and the teachers were 'strimenes' (loosely translated as 'twisted Aussie bitches').

Greek dancing never seemed to be a problem. Funny that. My brother played violin; I didn't get to play an instrument, because I would quit like my brother did. He got to play soccer, but I didn't get to, because it would affect my grades and schoolwork. It was obviously going to happen to me because that's what happened to my brother. The shorts/skirts were always a little too short for the girls that played sports, too.

GOOD LITTLE GREEK GIRL

"Only girls that want boys' attention, or are lesbians, play sports. Sports are for boys anyway. You don't want muscly legs like a man, do you? Yuk."

Guess why I never went to the gym and never wanted to work out or do cardio? Was I going to be vain? Was I going to look like a man? Was I going to be a lesbian? Was I going to the gym to be a slut?

I thought I was finally getting my reward for being such a good girl when I turned 19 years old.

That's when I met my first husband. I got married when I was 20 years old. We only dated for a very short time. I had my 21st six months after my wedding. I was already miserable but compliant because I did love my husband very much. He was my first serious boyfriend. He was my first everything.

I had my own list. I had the nifi points and now I was going to marry a good Greek boy and live happily ever after!

For God's sake, so delusional.

I was so easily manipulated in the real world, but I was happy to be making everyone else happy. Were they proud of me, now? Did they love me, now? Are you going to save me and get me away from these crazy people?

I'm a married woman now. Surely, that means things will change and I will finally be seen as an adult. Surely, my parents would back the fuck off now. I'm a married woman,

TO BE WORTHY

I'm an adult! I'll be the boss of my own life now. Just me and my husband.

I finally reached 'Wifey' status. Now my life was my own... Right?

Nope.

Chapter 3

The Wedding March vs 'Jaws' Theme Music

GOOD LITTLE GREEK GIRL

Let that *'Jaws'* soundtrack play in your head for a minute. Dun dun dun, dun deh dun… dun deh dun… They sound the same to me… Equally evoking fear.

I met my first husband at a Greek event at a night club. I had to fight with my parents to go. My curfew was 11pm. Literally when the club scene started to kick off. They took the fun out of it. They guilted me for dressing *"slutty"* with my jeans and a one shoulder top. I was 18. My parents always commented on my outfit and made me super uncomfortable and self-conscious.

I hated my body. I hated them. They guilted me for wanting to dance. They guilted me for wasting money. They assumed I was being a slut, other why else would someone go clubbing, right?

"What do you do there for that many hours? You don't dance the whole time?"

That is why they wanted me home. They decided that I had enough time to dance, and I was still out, I must be up to no good. Totally logical, right?

They would call, and call, and call. Then when I got sick of answering, in the club, music blaring, they would call my friends. Imagine being out at night with your friends, who were all at least five years my senior, and their parents are fast asleep, but your parents are doing the full circle stalker check call?

So overbearing. So overprotective. So embarrassing and degrading.

What did they think I was doing? Did they not know me at all? Did they not trust me?

They obviously thought very little of me. I had never given them any reason to accuse me of anything. Yet somehow they were sure that I was up to no good.

I felt like shit! I hated my life. I hated my parents. They were always so strict. Always so accusatory and degrading. Always so offended and offensive. Oppressive. Miserable.

But this was/is who they are. They don't know any better.

"They did the best they can."

I'm going to scream if I hear that one more time. They are still the same. A quick reminder: I was in my 40s when I wrote this, still the same fucking shit going down.. What a joke, total bullshit excuses. How the fuck did they not evolve with the rest of the world?

I digress…

So, I met him. He was Greek, so of course, my parents were happy. They were still happy when his family pushed for a super quick engagement and marriage. They would say stuff like, *"If you are a good girl, why do you want to wait to get married?"*

I had no hesitation because I was a *"good girl"* and I didn't want anyone to think I was not *nifi* material. After all, this was my great escape and my parents were encouraging it. It felt too good to be true. And it was.

GOOD LITTLE GREEK GIRL

The next nugget of wisdom was, *"You don't need to go to college anymore, you're a wife now. A wife needs to support her husband. You will work for the family business. Besides, you won't have time to work and study and have children."*

I had the chance to visit America for a few months, to work in my field with underprivileged children. An absolute dream career goal.

My parents disagreed.

I was not allowed to go to America. I was shattered. They didn't trust me. They were so consumed by what people would say if I travelled without my parents or a husband? They controlled everything. It still breaks my heart. I'm still so angry they denied me that experience. That was over 20 years ago. It still hurts.

Chapter 4

My Own Big Fat Greek Wedding

GOOD LITTLE GREEK GIRL

350 guests. I knew probably 70 of them.

Wedding party of 10. We had to have even numbers from my side and his side. The bridesmaid's and my gowns were all tailormade. The suits were tailored. We hired a caterer that would make traditional Greek village, wedding food. We hired a decorator that transformed the hall into a ballroom in a castle. It was beautiful, but none of it was me.

I had gone along with everything everyone else wanted. I felt like an outsider at my own wedding. I was numb. I was having a strange out of body experience. The morning of, my dad asked me if I really wanted to get married. I couldn't believe it. I wanted to say no, but could I?

Everyone would hate me. They had paid so much money! What would happen if I pulled out now? Everyone would think I was crazy and that would also mean I wasn't a good girl if I didn't want to get married. It was all so rushed. It was all too much. But too late.

My in-laws literally expected me pregnant upon our return from the honeymoon! My mother-in-law made no effort to hide her disgust to find out I was on the pill. She proudly announced that she went through my underwear draw in my bedroom to find them. She told me that I was going to get sick and get a hump back and ruin my body and get cancer if I didn't stop taking the pill straight away.

What the hell, lady?

MY OWN 'BIG FAT GREEK WEDDING'

Despite such a *warm welcome* to the family, I did everything they asked – except stop taking the pill. That was the only thing I had control over.

We bought our first house, but were not allowed to live in it. It was my father-in-law's idea that we should rent it out. That sounded reasonable, even if I wasn't thrilled about it. Then we would live in the back of the shop. No need to be late to work, now.

The house we bought was directly across the road from the shop. The only difference was that it wasn't physically attached i.e. not close enough for them to monitor us. If we lived in the house, we would have our own husband and wife time.

What newlyweds want privacy? Clearly not us.

If we lived in our house, all the way across the road, how would my mother-in-law have easy access to our bedroom so she could go through my private draws to assess the absence of pregnancy? She needed to know why I wasn't pregnant yet, because it was totally her call and her decision to make, right? Not mine or my husbands.

If we lived in our house, maybe the cord wouldn't reach, and she'd have to finally cut it. How would her son survive without her? He was a 23-year-old mamma's boy. I'm sure she kept his balls in her apron pocket, along with house keys and wads of cash from her illegitimate fruit stall. Tax, what's tax?

GOOD LITTLE GREEK GIRL

"This all cash money business. Is mine, not bloody goverrrnment."

That was her favourite saying. Imagine it in her heavy Greek accent. Roll those rrrr's baby.

Anyway, a lot of shit went down and I kept bitting my tongue. Repeating the patterns I had grown up with. Listening and nodding my head in agreeance, even if I was dying inside. At least I was married, right?

Until…

Chapter 5

Fuck You and Yo' Mamma!

GOOD LITTLE GREEK GIRL

We were invited for dinner. Nothing unusual. We only saw them, worked with them all day every day, of course we couldn't have dinner alone. We ate dinner with them almost every night as well.

This was the night they thought they would let me know... They were on to me!

Queue dramatic music...... Da da daaaaahhhhh!!!

They said they had been *keeping an eye* on me. They went through our trash and found receipts. Literal receipts. *Mikasa, Myer* etc. We had bought some friends a wedding and engagement gift. With our credit card. That we had in our own name. That we paid off ourselves, not from the family business.

Their natural conclusion was that *I alone*, had stolen money from the business and gone shopping.

I apparently, also wrote myself cheques. The cheques had to be co-signed, and all the stubs were for the cigarette company, the petrol company and my father-in-law's gambling debts.

Clearly the most logical conclusion was that I was a thief. This is why the business wasn't making money. Everyone forgot that my sister-in-law wrote herself a cheque and ran away from home for a few months, until the money ran out..

Oh, I also allegedly had an affair with the milk delivery guy. Yep. I went down to open the door for him one morning and moved a few things out of the way so he could get through with his loaded trolley, and in that 30 seconds, I fucked his brains out. Only logical explanation, right? Why else was I out of sight for 30 seconds?

That was the night I finally stood up for myself. I had moved from one control freak parenting situation to an even worse control freak parenting situation. I'd had enough.

I stood up and looked each one of them square in the eye, one by one.

"First of all, fuck you! Second of all, I come from a good family. You didn't find me in a gutter somewhere. You treat me like I came from nothing and I've been kissing your ass all these years, and you treat me like I still owe you. I owe you nothing! Everything has been done your way. And now, you call me a thief and a slut to top it off?"

Not my finest moment but it was the most genuine, infiltered thing that had ever come out of my mouth. I turned to my husband, who was in the corner, arms folded staring at the ground, silent as a mouse.

'As for you, you can either man up and come with your wife, or you can stay here with mummy and daddy and let them run the rest of your life. But I won't be in it."

I should have felt so liberated and happy and free, but I was numb. Not these days though. I always laugh my head off when I tell people the story now. I am quite proud of myself.

My adrenaline was though the roof. I went back to our room and I packed my stuff. I called my parents and told them to come get me. I was 23 and still didn't have my license or my own car. What did I need a license for? I didn't go anywhere by myself..

I had that super human strength. Picked up the heaviest suitcase and packed the car. I was not spending another minute there.

My dad let us live in one of his empty rentals. We lived together, in peace, like a real married couple for a while. Maybe a month or so. It was awesome!

Then one day he went and ruined it all by asking, *"When are you going to apologise?"*

"Are you kidding me? What did you just say?"

We had a huge fight and then he apologised. He said that we would have to work it out. He couldn't understand how we were all going to get over this, so we can get along when they want to spend time with our children. It was finally time to say what I had been putting off.

"I don't want to have their grandbabies, ever. I don't want to have kids if they are going to be part of their life and upbringing. I don't want people like that influencing how my children grow up. I hate your parents and what they did to you guys and what they did to me. I know your parents will want to control everything we do and I won't have it. I want my kids to finish school. Not get pulled out so they can work.

I want my kids to go to Tafe or uni, even if they are girls. I want them to have the choice to decide, at least. I want to live with my kids, knowing we have our own separate lives, not having to do everything with your parents all the time. I don't want to keep asking them for their permission. I want to be a grown up with a grown up husband."

He pretended to agree with me.

He then calmly asked me to go out with him to another Greek night. Similar to the one at which we first met. He said that even if we get a divorce that I will always be the love of his life and his best friend. He said he will never fall in love again and he didn't think he would ever find a wife like me. I was the best wife anyone could ask for and he couldn't ask for more.

Why didn't he defend me then? Why did he stay silent in the corner? Was I supposed to believe him?

I had to think about it. I was so hurt and embarrassed and ashamed and angry.

Anyway, we went out and had a few drinks and enjoyed the night together, like when we were first dating. The next thing I knew, I was awake. Naked. Dizzy as hell.

And had the most intense discharge I've even seen in my life. I could not stop vomiting. I only have a few glasses of wine. Not enough to be so sick.

I went to the doctor and had a few tests. I had opioids in my system. The same sort that his mother took to her help sleep.

GOOD LITTLE GREEK GIRL

I got the morning after pill. No babies for you, you sick fucks.

Did you know that's called *date rape* even if you're married? I thought that was really strange. Comical. But then again, I always made shitty situations into funny ones.

The funniest part I remember was when I got home after the doctors. I was like the *'Incredible Hulk'*. We had a 12,foot tinnie parked in the back yard at the end of our driveway. I single handedly pulled it down our driveway and parked it right in front of the stairs at the front of the house.

From the landing at the top of the stairs, I was throwing his clothes, speakers, jewellery, shoes, fishing gear, torches... anything that was his that I wanted gone with him.

He pulled up. I met him outside. I asked him, *"Did we have sex last night?"*

His smug smile said it all, *"Would it matter if we did? We are married."*

I told him he was a sicko.

I told him to hook up his boat and go back to mummy and daddy. I was positive they were in on this masterplan. That was their obsession through our whole marriage, me getting pregnant. Trapping me.

In their mind, I would never leave if I was pregnant. I have a feeling they would have fought me for full custody if I had a baby.

I got a DVO and filed for divorce. It took three years to finalise. I was left with enough money to buy a car and go on a holiday.

I figured a nice holiday would be nice to help regain my sanity. I booked tickets to Greece. I was going to do whatever I wanted. I was going to have some peace and quiet. Sleep, eat, beach..

Again, my parents disagreed...

Chapter 6

The Aftermath

GOOD LITTLE GREEK GIRL

The realisation was debilitating. What was it all for? What did it get me? What had I lost by not following my heart and pursuing my dreams. Where did I stand now? What was I in the eyes of God and other people? What was I worth?

I was certain it was nothing.

Fuck my life.

I hated the world and everyone in it. How could I do everything right and still fail so miserably? I was the perfect good little Greek girl. I cooked, I cleaned, I did everything my parents told me to. I did everything my husband and his parents wanted me to. Except have kids, thank God. I didn't deserve this shit. It was so unfair. There were so many other people that did less than me that looked so much happier. Luckier.

I never understood rock bottom. I thought I'd hit it a few times but then fell even lower.

Now What? I was used, damaged goods.

Do the only other thing I'm good at – bury myself in work. Make money. I was sure I'd work out the rest later. I didn't have a plan, just survive for now.

I decided to do a fast, track hairdressing course. That'll do. I can do that. I was so lost. I didn't know what to do but I didn't want to work in cafes all the time. I didn't finish my study, and I felt too dumb to go back and study gain. I was too broken to go back and further my studies.

I wanted to be a phycologist. I felt like a hypocrite. How can someone that messed up so much at life, help others? Who was I to give advice to anyone?

I had to live with my parents. They would not let me live alone. What would people say? Unmarried and living alone? Oh, the shame!

I ended up house sitting my brother's house for a while. Then I rented a room from my friend for a while. The timeline is a little fuzzy between 2003 and 2007. I just know I was busy!

I eventually decided I needed a plan. A way to keep going forward – or I'd kill myself. Those were simply my only two options. I took that holiday.

My parents followed me to Greece.

They hijacked my serenity. The only chance I gave myself to heal.

They booked all three tickets, so we had to travel together. I couldn't even escape them on the plane. 24 hours straight, listening to them bicker and complain and watch them flounder over simple tasks. Getting our passports out. Lining up through security. Filling out the declaration forms.

Just like every other time we left the house as a family, I would have to step up and be the parent and show them how to do stuff in the real world, outside their little bubble. Of course, I had to babysit them and tell them how to act right, but do it from a position of the daughter, that didn't know anything.

Super contradicting but I always had to be so gentle with them and let them feel like they thought of it or they already knew it.

"Do we need our passports now? What did you put on your form? I think they said to do it like this? Are we supposed to line up here with everyone else?"

Once we reached our accommodation, I slept for three days! I was exhausted, mentally, emotionally, physically.

The villagers asked them if I was mentally sound. Why else would a grown woman be travelling with her parents and literally stuck together, day and night? I gladly set the record straight.

I was not the mentally unstable one, they would not leave me in peace. Stuck to me like dog shit on my shoe. I just wanted some peace!

They wouldn't let me stay in a hotel. I had to stay in a family house with them. NO privacy. No mosquito nets. No air con. But why would I stay in a hotel? What was I going to get up to in a hotel? Didn't matter, what were people going to *think* I did in a hotel by myself?

I wasn't allowed to rent a car. I started walking to the beach one day. My dad got in the car and in true psycho style, yelled at me through the car window, *"Get in the car Eleni! Now! Before people see you walking around by yourself!"* gritting his teeth.

THE AFTERMATH

I was so angry that I didn't want to spend another day with them in the house, watching them do laundry. We were literally on an island and weren't going to the beach. Make it make sense, please.

You can't make this shit up…

They didn't want me going anywhere, until one of my friends brothers said I was pretty. Then they were waking me at 11pm to go out with this girl I did not know, so I could meet this boy. That would solve all their problems. I would be married again. No one asked what I wanted. Besides, I wasn't exactly single at that time..

I was tired. I was on holidays. Before I left Australia, I was working two jobs, 16-hour days. I needed a holiday. My divorce stress was exacerbated due to my parents meddling and trying to control everything. I had a nervous breakdown. I was not well. I lost 10kg in roughly two to three weeks.

I finally escaped to a *Contiki* tour and I had the time of my life. My first taste of real freedom. My mum wanted to come with me. Thank God it had an age cut off. I didn't enjoy the partying or drinking, I enjoyed the peace, the quiet, the respect of the others around me.

For the first time in my life, I was being treated as an equal. People weren't talking over me. People were asking me questions and they were genuinely interested in me.

Chapter 7

Racist to the Core

GOOD LITTLE GREEK GIRL

I wish my family weren't so racist. The opportunities I missed just because my friends and the one boy I actually had feelings for weren't Greek.

My best friend was Turkish. Even though they liked her as a person, they couldn't see past the fact that she was Turkish. She was just a kid. We were only 16 years old. We had so much in common.

She was my first real best friend that I hung out with after school. Of course I had to lie and tell my parents it was a group class project. It wasn't a compete lie. We did about 20 minutes of schoolwork and then hung out for a couple of hours.

It was through this friend that I met my first love.

He was my age. We instantly had a connection. The only thing that was *wrong* with him, he wasn't Greek. He came from a good family of Catholic faith. He even said he would convert to Orthodox, just to be with me because he knew my parents were opposed to us being together. He said he would learn Greek. He invited me to his school formal. I had to beg and fight with my parents to go.

I went but I ended up breaking his heart on an otherwise beautiful night. He asked me again to be his girlfriend. I was so terrified of my parents, I said no. It broke my heart as much as it did his. I just knew that if he was my boyfriend, my parents would never let me see him.

At least as friends, I could still have him in my life and I could still see him. It was so hard because we had strong feelings for each other. To this day, we haven't even kissed. I couldn't bring myself to because then it would be far too emotional and that line would have been crossed. I still feel a twin flame connection whenever I think of him.

It wasn't just my parents, it was uncles and aunties, too. My godmother said to me, *"You don't want him to be the only black person at the table, do you? Your kids will look different to the rest of the family."*

Diversity apparently was unacceptable.

I forced myself to distance myself from my love. It was too painful to both of us to be so connected but disconnected at the same time. My parents had gone as far as threatening to disown me and take me out of the will.

I started to notice other boys. I liked one of my brother's friends. I was never going to act on it but I had to find myself a distraction from the forbidden union.

I hadn't spoken to or seen him in months. I was concentrating on forgetting about him. Then out of nowhere, my parents invited him to attend an event. Where the new boy I liked also was. We were in a fashion parade together.

My parents were fucking with my emotions and my head. Did they really think so little of me and disregard my emotions that they thought they could just make me flick them on and off?

GOOD LITTLE GREEK GIRL

Why were they so cruel? I had been forcing myself to hate him. I was looking for things that I could hold against him. Now my parents were just like it's okay now. You can like him again.

How did they see this going in their head? And how long was this going to last for? Were they going to monitor every time I saw him now? Were they going to let me date him properly?

I was almost 18 years old by then. It took that long for them to come around. Three years of crying, begging, longing, missing him.

It was torture.

Chapter 8

Great Grandmother's Curse: We Didn't Learn?

GOOD LITTLE GREEK GIRL

I've been hearing snippets of this story for years. But it was a big family secret because it was so scandalous. The people that were feeding the shame of the story was our own family. It was the reaction of the family that made this story more about how it would affect them, instead of what it could teach us and how we could grow from it. Instead, we buried it and we let it control generations negatively.

They gave way too much power to the family *shame*. I don't see it as a story of shame, I see it as a story of how devastating life can be when we give others too much control over our own happiness.

My great-grandmother fell in love with a widower. They were in love and engaged to be married. They were waiting to receive the blessing from the priest to get married as my great-grandfather had been married before, and although his first wife has passed away, they were still married by the church.

In Orthodox weddings, you are married by law and you are also married by the church, so when a marriage ends, you have to also have a church divorce.

They were already married in every sense of the word, except for having the official ceremony. They living together, engaged, and she was already raising his children from his previous marriage and pregnant with their child together. That baby was my grandfather.

One day, my great-grandmother went to find the priest as she had waited so long for him, she had given birth and my grandfather was around two years old. This saga had obviously dragged on for years, and the poor lady was seen as a tramp with a bastard baby.

What sin had this woman committed? She was taking care of children as her own. She was in love and in a committed relationship. She was begging to do the right thing and have the right thing done by her and her baby. There was no scandal. There was just judgment and too much power in the wrong hands.

My great-grandmother ended up committing the greatest 'sin' of all. Suicide. But, this was on the advice of the priest she had gone to see. The priest that was holding up the formal process of her marriage.

He told her that she was not worthy of the blessing and no one would ever accept her as she was a tramp. She hung herself on a tree on her way home. That tree was known to the local villagers as *her* tree. I have kept the name private as to protect my family, but if you know, you know. Everyone on the island they lived on in Greece knew the story.

How could a man of God be so spiteful and hateful and judgmental? The man that preaches love and forgiveness. The one that preaches about Mary Magdeline. His personal agenda overrode the word of God and sent her to her death.

When I finally heard the full story, my first reaction was, *"Fuck this shit! How can he do that?"*

Then I got really angry.

GOOD LITTLE GREEK GIRL

My whole life was dictated by what others thought, when really, after that happened to my great-grandmother, I just would have gone the opposite way. I would have said, not me, not today or ever.

Instead, the whole family retreated to shame. Even the generations after. They gave the stigma so much power for single mothers, unwed mothers. Yet where was the man's role in the same scenario. Irrelevant. All the shame and guilt lands on the lady.

The family still complains about how my grandfather was treated, but no one says anything to the people that need to hear it. They just keep repeating the narrative to the same circle of people that won't ever do anything to change it.

Because no one wanted to put their neck on the line, my grandfather was written out of his family's will. His own siblings and cousins disowned him but would still sit at the table and share meals with the very man that they disowned.

How does that make sense? The hierarchy at its finest.

Despite the betrayal, we all went along and attended each other's weddings and children's weddings and christenings. If I had known then what I know now, I would have boycotted. I have no interest in pretending and respecting those who do not respect me.

This is exactly how I got myself written out of my other grandfather's will. I don't want anything from you if you're a shit person.

GREAT GRANDMOTHER'S CURSE: WE DIDN'T LEARN?

My other grandfather was an adulterer, abuser of every kind and a very evil, unkind man.

As soon as I was old enough to realise what he was, I never spoke to him again. I would end up face to face with him at family functions and I would look at him as a stranger and would carry on as if I did not know him. No hello. No hugs. No fake bullshit.

A man who hits his wife even in her 70s, manipulates, steals and cheats? No thanks. I do not want you anywhere near me.

My heart grew even colder when I heard what my father had to endure as a baby because of him.

I could have played the game and ended up getting a cut of his will, but I made peace early on, knowing that it wasn't worth it.

I would not have a relationship of any kind with this demon.

Chapter 9

Umm... That's Not Normal

I grew up watching my father make the money and my mother doing everything else. My mother had the mother-in-law from hell. Her father-in-law was the devil himself. I don't refer to them as my grandparents because I've never had that relationship with them. They were people that I knew through my father. That's it.

She was always rushing to get home before Dad, hoping to avoid the arguments, the accusations. Yet she was the one that was forgiving infidelity. Forgiving abuse. She had learnt responses to avoid conflict. My father has always been extremely controlling. Not much has changed over the years, except that now not much slides now without me or Mum fighting back.

I grew up thinking so many things were normal. I now know that they are all forms of domestic abuse.

1. Isolating you from your support system
A controlling partner will try to cut you off from friends and family or limit contact with them, so you don't receive the support you need.

My father used to lock the *Telecom* phone we had so Mum couldn't call anyone when he wasn't home. She had to take two babies to the hairdresser across the road if we needed to call the doctor. My mother also had no transport. She had to call her father to come and pick us up if we needed to go to anywhere while Dad was at work.

Later, when she was *allowed* to use the phone, he would go through the bill and question all the numbers she had dialled and then questioned the timing of each call. He still obsesses over letters that are addressed to her and hovers until he finds out who the letter is from and what it says. He still hates it when she receives notifications on her phone.

2. Monitoring your activity throughout the day
My father and husband would do this. Wanting a breakdown of the day. What time, how long, who with, what time you left, how long it took you to get home, calculating what time you should be due home and questioning if you weren't home when expected.

3. Denying you freedom and autonomy
Someone exerting coercive control might try to control your freedom of movement and independence. Some methods include:

- Not allowing you to go to work or complaining when you do. Dad and my ex always complained about our work taking priority over the domestic duties and their personal care. They act like incapable children and sulk as if they had been abandoned, left to suffer and fend for themselves.
- Restricting your access to transportation. Mum didn't have her own car until I was in second grade. My ex would leave me without a vehicle for days when he decided to go hunting with friends. His vehicle would sit in the driveway, but I couldn't drive it.

4. Gaslighting
The abuser must always be right and they will force the victim to acknowledge this. They'll manipulate, lie, and gaslight to

get their way and convince you that you're wrong. You are wrong even when you are agreeing with them. Sometimes, it's just about you being wrong. Just to degrade you. I've seen this and lived it so many times.

I can't tell you how many times I find myself questioning my own memory, apologising, and regretting starting a conversation or asking a question.

5. Name-calling and putting you down
Malicious put-downs, name-calling, and frequent criticisms are all forms of bullying behaviour. They're designed to make you feel unimportant and deficient.

I learnt so many disgusting insults from my father. None I would repeat but I did think it was normal to be spoken to like that. They lose so much in translation but they were something along the lines of:

- *"Why are you barking like a dog? Shut up and stop barking like a dog."*
- *"Baby-brained bitch."*
- *"Do it again/say it again and I'll put you on the ground and step on your throat."*
- *"I'm going to strangle you/decapitate you."*
- *"Who were you being a whore with?"*
- *"I'm going to smash your fucking face in."*

You get the gist. Imagine you're talking to an animal you absolutely despise. I wouldn't even talk to an animal that way.

6. Limiting your access to money
Controlling finances is a way of restricting your freedom and ability to leave the relationship. Some ways they'll try to exert financial control include:

Placing you on a strict budget that barely covers the essentials, such as food or clothes. There is always a question on what the money is needed for. Always make you feel so unappreciative and unreasonable and selfish, even when buying groceries for the household.

Limiting your access to bank accounts. It's so typical that men in our culture have multiple bank accounts that their wife can't access, assuming she even knows about it.

Hiding financial resources, secret bank accounts and cash.

Preventing you from having a credit card. Terrified that you might run away if you have the means. Or spend it on something selfish.

Rigorously monitoring what you spend, going through bank statements and questioning transactions, even if they are from the local supermarket.

7. Reinforcing traditional gender roles
Regardless of the type of relationship you have, your partner may try to make a distinction between who functions as the man and the woman in the relationship.

They'll attempt to justify that women are homemakers and mothers, while men are the breadwinners. Using this argument, they may coerce you into taking care of all the cleaning, cooking, and childcare. My ex told me to just take care of the house but when I wasn't working/earning, I would always have to listen to him complain about money and how he is doing everything and I'm not contributing.

8. Turning your kids against you
If you have children, either with the abuser or someone else, they may try to weaponize the children against you by telling them you're a bad parent or belittling you in front of them. My ex told my daughter that she's going to be so disappointed in me when she's old enough to realise what I've done to him.

This attitude can create a rift in the relationship between you and your kids and may make you feel powerless. My daughter felt so confused and betrayed.

9. Controlling aspects of your health and body
They'll monitor and control how much you eat, sleep, or time you spend in the bathroom.

Your abuser may require you to count calories after every meal or adhere to a strict exercise regimen. They may also control which medications you're allowed to take and whether you go for medical care or not.

Every time I would start a diet, my ex would force feed me chocolate, or a cookie or something he knew would hinder my efforts. Insisting that I take at least one bite.

He also shamed me for taking pain medications and anti-anxiety medication. He started to tell anyone that listened that I was abusing my prescription medication and *Nurofen*. He pushed me to switch to medicinal cannabis, but I later realised he was trying to set me up as he would request a drug test. Trying anything to prove I'm an unfit mother.

He told everyone I was an alcoholic. Everyone was starting to make comments and monitoring me. A casual glass of wine at dinner was feeding the rumour.

The smear campaign started long ago. It's still going and now my brother and his wife and joined my ex's mission.

Dad is always complaining about how much money Mum spends on physio. She has a lot of back, neck and shoulder pain. He used to always say to her, *"Are you still eating?"* or *"Are you eating again?"*

These days it's a more subtle jab like, *"I'm not eating, I haven't done enough to get hungry today. If you don't move all day, you shouldn't be hungry. Are you going to eat?"*

You may feel as though you're always walking on eggshells and that your body is no longer your own, all day every day.

10. Making jealous accusations
Jealously complaining about the amount of time you spend with your family and friends, both on and offline, is a way for them to phase out and minimise your contact with the outside world.

They might also do this in an effort to make you feel guilty. This includes time spent at work or on work related projects.

I can't tell you how many times I've heard, *"You're on your phone again?"*

"Are you still laying down?"

"Why are you doing that for them (work)?"

"Do you have to go?"

"Just quit and the care of the house. You hate it there anyway. I'm sick of hearing about your work. You don't even bring much money home, it's no use working."

11. Regulating your sexual relationship
Abusers might make demands about the amount of times you have sex each week and the kinds of activities you perform. They may also demand to take sexual pictures or videos of you or refuse to wear a condom.

You know that saying, *"If a man doesn't get what he wants at home, he'll go get it somewhere else."* That's what my husband told me the week before I left. I was still healing from surgery and I was not in a good place, physically or emotionally.

"Tell me what we're doing because I have to do what I need to do."

I'm assuming that had something to do with his new girlfriend. I felt like she'd been in the picture for a long time..

12. Threatening your children or pets

If physical, emotional, or financial threats don't work as desired, your abuser may try to use threats against others in an attempt to control you. For example, your kids or pets may be at risk. This can look like:

- Making violent threats against them like, *"Come sort out your daughter before I do."*
- Threatening to call social services and say you're neglecting or abusing your children when you aren't.
- Intimidating you by threatening to make important decisions about your kids without your consent.
- Threatening to kidnap your children. He said he was taking my daughter out of the state to live with his parents.
- Threatening to get rid of your pet. There were constant threats if my daughter and I hadn't picked up dog poo etc. He would kick him. The dog was so small he would fly a few feet away.

Coercive control is a deeply harmful and insidious form of abuse. It can be hard to recognize at first because it's often subtle. control, and constant surveillance. These behaviours gradually strip away your independence, self-esteem, and sense of safety, making it feel almost impossible to leave.

Importantly, having some happy memories with the abuser doesn't negate the abuse. Many abusers use intermittent kindness or affection as part of the control – it's a tactic, not a justification.

GOOD LITTLE GREEK GIRL

No one deserves to be manipulated, controlled, or made to feel small or scared in their own life or relationship.

That's why I'm mindful of what my daughter learns from me.

My dad asked me one day, *"Am I an asshole? Have I been an asshole?"*

I had to be honest, *"You know you have, Dad. You still are sometimes."*

His ego took control of the conversation and he replied, *"Yeah, but that's why you're good kids now!?"*

"No Dad, that's not how it works."

If he was hard on us to make us good kids, then why was he so horrible to Mum?

I remember comforting Mum as she cried on the couch. She was crying because Dad was having affairs and she was being pressured into taking him back. She was being told that a single mother was a wasted woman and she would be alone forever. No other man would ever want her or her children. She would be rejected by the community. An outcast.

How did she become the bad guy?

I watch my dad tower over my mum when they fought, his face bright red, teeth gritting, his eyeballs bulging, and she was pinned back to the wall. I used to run away but one day I started screaming at him and pulling him away.

I can't tell you how many times I ended up in my room, back up against the door, feet digging into the carpet and my entire body throwing weight back on to the door so Dad couldn't come in. I was in survival mode. I had no fear, just anger and hatred and the strength of 20 men.

The only thing stopping my dad from pushing on the other side of the door was the sound of the timber door cracking ever so slightly. Lucky he loved the house, otherwise there'd be no stopping him. He always had to win.

He once fractured a bone in my hand. I was playing around pretending to do karate chops. Instead of playing along and just tapping me, blocking me whatever, he got competitive and forceful. When I told him he hurt me, he just said, *"Don't be stupid. I was just playing. I couldn't have hurt you. If it hurts, just shake it off."*

I listened after some protest and tried to shake my hand thinking he knew what he was talking about, because he had done karate for years and had probably seen injuries before. I probably just had to shake the thumb back into place.

Utter agony…

It definitely made it worse. I begged him to take me to the doctor or hospital, but he refused. Didn't have the time or money and he was positive that he did no wrong. He still thinks he can do no wrong.

Mum came home and took me straight to the doctor. I had to wear a cast for six weeks. His ego was more important to him than letting a kid play fight, more important than admitting he may have gone too far and done something wrong.

We had a lot of violent, loud fights at home. I was at the bottle shop across the road from our house one time, speaking with the guy that worked there. I was asking him to show me where to find the wine my dad wanted and brought up in conversation that I lived across the road. The guy froze for a second. Then he asked with caution:

"Which house? There is always screaming and fighting coming from that house over there."

He pointed to my home. I said we were further down on the next block. I held back the tears, but I think he knew I was lying. I paid and left as quickly as possible. We were the neighbourhood psychopaths that everyone had noticed and were talking about our house of horrors.

Always watched my mum have a break down and scream and cry before we had guests over. Always watched her go way above and beyond as if the queen was coming. Everyone was so judgmental. But no one judged her as harshly as she judged herself. She had so much to prove to everyone. Everyone was so mean and critical and hypocritical.

As I got older, I would always tell her that everything was good enough. She is still resistant to doing things differently, still scared of conflict and judgement.

Now she is so bitter. Anxiety and stress fucks you up, mentally, emotionally and physically. Her nerves are so shot, she can't get in a car without crying. She has to drive and she drives 15km-20km under the limit, practically stopping to turn corners etc.

She gave all of herself and now she has nothing left.

I want her to be free and I don't even care if I get the blame for it. I'll be blamed for encouraging them to divorce. That'll be my fault too somehow, but I won't even care because they might actually be happy.

I watched my father get angry at her, yelling at her and asking why everything wasn't ready yet. Instead of helping her and supporting her, he screamed at her and put her down. All he had to do was start the fire, set the tables up and put ice in the esky. I thought that was normal. The man does the outside stuff and everything else was done by the lady.

Chapter 10

Just Like the Movies

GOOD LITTLE GREEK GIRL

I have watched a million movies in my life. Straight away, everyone thinks of *'My Big Fat Greek Wedding'* but I also think of movies like *'The Croods'*.

'The Croods' are a neanderthal family. 'Grug' is the strong, protective patriarch of the family, which sounds lovely, until you realise he is so resistant to change, he is hurting his family. They live by the code, *"Never not be afraid,"* because fear of danger keeps them alive.

This resonated with me so much, honestly, I cried. The mother follows the father blindly, supporting her husband and forcing the kids to follow the rules. They lock themselves in a cave all night and the only come out during the day to eat. The daughter 'Eep', seeks adventure as she doesn't want to just wait until they die. They are so worried about dying, they refuse to live. The main message is to thrive, not just survive.

> *"That's not living, that's just not dying!"*
> (The Croods, 2013)

They learn to embrace change and learn to listen to their children by the end of the movie. We also learn:

1. Parents aren't always right.
2. Self-talk is a powerful thing.
3. Try to see things from someone else's perspective.
4. Facing our fears helps those around us.
5. Have the courage to believe in yourself.

I also love comedians like Joe Koi, Anthony Rodea, Sooshi Mango. I know they aren't Greek, but they share so many relatable situations. We can laugh about it now but that shit wasn't funny when we were growing up.

Chapter 11

I'm So Tired, But That Never Stopped Me

GOOD LITTLE GREEK GIRL

Just before I set off on my big, expensive, once in a lifetime, dream, nightmare, stressful, exhausting, holiday, I met someone that would shape the next 17 years of my life – and also gift me the absolute light of my life, my daughter.

So, I was divorced.

The stress of getting divorced was not too bad. The one thing that made me lose my mind were my parents. They were so in my face about everything.

My mother would call me and hound me on the daily. She once called me while I was at work. I hung up a few times then answered, thinking it might be something important for one. She was just asking for an update, again!

"Did you call your lawyer? What's happening? What did he say?"

Then the endless whining and complaining and bitching and bringing up the past and then comparing it to her own miserable existence.

Lady, you're not helping.

Stop harassing me. Stop winding me up, especially when I'm trying to work. I was on edge all day every day. I couldn't deal with thinking about it, reliving it, talking about it. I took so much energy to be present in the moment and pretend I didn't wish I was dead.

I'M SO TIRED, BUT THAT NEVER STOPPED ME

Work was my safe place. My happy place. The more I worked, the happier I was. Totally disconnected and disassociated. Unhealthy but it worked for me.

My parents still don't get it. They are extremely emotionally immature. Even with my current divorce, they keep asking me what my plan is. How long it's going to take and how much is it going to cost? How the hell am I supposed to know that? These are obviously their priorities. I'm trying to get them to understand the most important thing to me and my daughter is our mental health and our emotional well-being. The money and time are irrelevant to me. I just want to protect my daughter and myself from the living hell I am all too familiar with.

Back to 2005, I was *surviving* with my parents. I was dating but had I an exit strategy for every relationship I started. I hated being trapped. I hated the idea of ever getting married again. I was so angry with everyone. I was angry at the world. I was sure everyone was going to hurt me so I was looking for things to break up with them over. Because the world is the way it is, It didn't take long to find something wrong with everyone I met.

Broke, alcoholic, misogynistic, smelly feet, bad breath, lived with his mum and over 30. Any reason would be good enough for me to break up with them, really. I was convinced that everyone was out to destroy me and hurt me, use me like my first husbands' family.

One guy picked me up for my birthday. He was two hours late. He took me to dinner but complained about the prices as soon as we sat down, so we didn't eat. We just got drinks. Then we ended up at the casino and he put $50 in a machine. That was it. He couldn't afford a meal, or a bunch of flowers or a birthday card, but he could afford a $50 at the casino? Next!

But there was still the old me that believed that I didn't want to be alone. Still that old niggling feeling that I was incomplete unless I was married and didn't have kids. I cried so many nights thinking I was going to be alone forever.

No one ever loved me and no one ever will. I wasn't good enough. I was stupid. I was too rough. I was too tomboy. I was too angry. I wasn't worth love. Had I lost my nifi points?

In 2007, I met my brother's friend. We'll call him Rory. He was older. He had a job. He had two kids. His parents were good people. He liked me. I think I hit the jackpot. Plus, he loved that I was such a good little Greek girl. That's what he loved the most.

Especially compared to his ex-wife, who was *"so lazy"*. She didn't keep a clean house. She didn't cook. She didn't appreciate that he was such a hard worker and couldn't understand that he was building his brother's house and working full time and renovating the house they were living in.

It wasn't his fault that she introduced him to drugs and that he turned to drugs to cope toward the end of their marriage. He was such a hero because he sent himself up north to work F.I.F.O and he stopped all the drugs, cold turkey.

Okay, so let's update that narrative.

In 2007, I met my brother's friend. He was older. He had a job. He had two kids. His parents were good people. He liked me. I think I hit the jackpot. Plus, he loved that I was such a good little Greek girl. That's what he loved the most.

Especially compared to his ex-wife, who was ~~so lazy!~~ overwhelmed.

She ~~wouldn't~~ couldn't keep a clean house. She ~~didn't~~ couldn't cook every night because she was studying and had two small children. She ~~didn't appreciate~~ was growing impatient, ~~that he was such a hard worker and couldn't understand that~~ as he was building his brother's house and working full time and renovating the house they were living in. She had two small children in a house that was barely liveable. It's just his style to rip everything out instead of working on one project/room at a time.

It ~~wasn't his fault that she introduced him to drugs and that he turned to~~ was his own decision to more frequently use drugs to cope, toward the end of their marriage. He was ~~such a hero because he sent himself up~~ ran away from his problems and travelled up north to work F.I.F.O and he stopped all the drugs, cold turkey, because they ran mandatory random drug and alcohol tests. He told me he sat in his donga for two weeks getting clean, but it's more realistic that he stayed in a hotel up north until he could pass his drug test. They don't let you stay in the dongas when you're not working. The employer has to pay rent for each donga and cleaners for each donga. Something I learnt much later.

GOOD LITTLE GREEK GIRL

So many lies/half-truths. I believed everything he said because I had no reason not to. Also, this guy seemed to worship me. He told me I was so much better than his ex. That's all I needed to feel like this was a perfect match. He understood the nifi points so it was all worth it once again. Plus, I wasn't going to be alone! I was worthy again. I was loved again. I wasn't *used goods*, anymore.

He was older and he had also been married and had kids. This was meant to be a grown, experienced man. Not a child, mamma's boy like my ex.

At the time we met, he wasn't close to his parents. That was a huge green flag for me because that meant he was the opposite of my ex. He was not talking to his brother. That means his brother was not going to be enmeshed into our relationship like my ex and his siblings. Another green flag.

I was so wrong.

I went to Greece in 2008, very soon after we met, and he went to see his family in a different country overseas at the same time. It was the most romantic gesture when he met me at one of my stops on my *Contiki* tour. We spent a few nights together, doing what lovers do. I thought I was so lucky. Yet I got a certain ick at the same time.

He told me that his ex-wife helped him book his holiday. She found out that he upgraded his room from a single to a double bed and she wanted to know why. I found out at that time that were not yet divorced, but separated and she was under the impression that there was still hope of reconciliation.

I got over that because he told me that she was delusional and that there was no way that they were getting back together. He just needed help booking his trip and used her credit card because he didn't have one. Apparently they were only still in touch and friends because of their kids. I believed it. She was just desperate and delusional, obviously. I knew that because he told me.

On the last night of our romantic rendezvous, he was acting a little strange but he told me he wasn't feeling well because of the food on the dinner cruise we were on. Looking back, I think he was fighting with his ex because he lied to her about where he was going and who with. Also, he was arranging to meet back up with his family on his return to the country he was visiting before our little meet up.

Now I know, he just came to check up on me and see who I was on tour with and make sure everyone understood I was taken. Meanwhile, on his camera there was a photo of him with his arm on a blonde girl's waist.

Excuse me?

Instead of just telling me who she was and apologising for putting his hand where it had no business being, he smashed his camera on the ground. Then he blamed me for making him mad with my accusations. He, however, had questioned me on every single guy in every photo I had on my camera. I wasn't even holding or being held by anyone. Just big group photos with a bunch of us leaning in. The people I was on tour with. There were about 50 of us, not including the driver and the tour guide.

GOOD LITTLE GREEK GIRL

We got back to Australia, moved in together and started living as a married couple in every sense, except the actual marriage.

I had worked two full time jobs, prior to meeting him. Eventually I started running my own business from 2010 until 2013.

I started the business from the ground up. A cafe in a small complex. I loved it! I had a lot of challenges with the landlord, 2010 flood, new tenants that were direct competition for my business etc.

The biggest challenge, however, was at home.

He hated that I was devoting so much time and energy into the new business. I was working seven days a week. It was a very rough start and I worked my ass off to make the business didn't tank in the first six months.

I had just completed the fit out, council licencing and approvals, menus, procedure manuals etc and was a week away from our grand opening, when the whole complex was completely wiped out by the flood. The water reached two foot about the ceiling. We lost everything.

I had a $50k business loan to pay off. The bank was holding $50k of my dad's money as a cash guarantee. I had a legal contract, a three year lease that I had to pay rent for. I had no option but to work my ass off and make this business work.

I'M SO TIRED, BUT THAT NEVER STOPPED ME

He resented me for it.

"All you care about is the shop!" he would yell.

My parents had bent over backwards, helping with the money for the shop, helping at the shop, helping me so we could save money on wages. They even let us live in one of their houses, rent free, so that we could get on our feet and save a deposit to buy our own home.

Remember this was after we had already been together for six years. He kept coming up with hardships and sob stories. I just kept trying to help him. Then I roped my parents in, and they were helping us. The more help we got, the more he backed off! The more he let us do and the more he expected from us.

It might have been easier to walk away from the business and work for someone else, but I wasn't ready to take that gamble. I was confident that I could make this business work, and it did!

I ran it successfully for the three years. So successfully in fact, that my landlord totally screwed me and refused to honour my additional two-year option on the lease. He started to show up every morning for breakfast. I thought it was very odd, but I could never imagine what he was up to.

He was running the numbers. He told me straight one day.

"I see you're really busy. It's very good. I counted, 26 large coffees, 12 regular, 16 small coffees since I got here today.

GOOD LITTLE GREEK GIRL

You sell them for $5.50 and $4.50 and $3.50? That's very good money. I was adding it up."

The cheeky prick. I was worried he was going to raise my rent. But it was worse...

"My friend wants this shop. When you leave, my friend will come in the shop."

Boom! My world imploded. All this work for nothing? She wasn't buying the business, she was just waiting for my lease to expire so she could move in. My landlord told me I could take him to court if I wanted to. I considered it but then I realised I would never win. He had it on record that I was in arrears on my rent, thus in breach of contract. How could this be?

When the flood hit in 2010, the landlord was not able to charge rent for the time that the centre was uninhabitable, by law. He told all the tenants that he gave us an extra month free that we were entitled to, out of the kindness of his heart. But this was his fallback plan to get rid of me. He asked where I had that documented in writing.

None of us had it writing. It was just a visit from the managing agent that spoke to me about the grace period. I had six months free already built into my contract. It was all very confusing and messy and that's the way the landlord preferred it.

Chapter 12

A Narc of My Own

GOOD LITTLE GREEK GIRL

Narcissistic abuse has been detrimental to my emotional, physical and mental health.

We had split between between 2013 and 2015. I was happily existing/surviving on my own, once again. During that time, I had buried myself in work again. I worked three jobs at once. I had saved $35k while we were separated and what we used for the deposit. We got back together late 2015 and bought a townhouse and planned to get pregnant.

I was hopeful that all the promises he made were going to come true. When the red flags started to appear again, I was convinced better the devil you know. I let a lot slide. I bit my tongue.

Another three years had passed and I had nothing but anxiety and PTSD to show for it. I was once told I was a walking stroke. My blood pressure was through the roof and my doctors were deeply concerned. I needed to make a change in my life as it was looking to be a short, not so sweet, one.

I have come through many family disputes, narcissistic abuse, sexual abuse, emotional abuse, physical abuse, mental abuse, chronic pain, chronic fatigue, spinal surgery and most recently, a brain tumour. I have learnt that my physical ailments are manifestations of my emotional and mental state.

Infidelity seemed to be a common theme in our relationship. Him always accusing me of cheating, but him actually being in places he had no business being in. Like topless bars and strip joints while I was pregnant. He would go out every

Friday for drink after work. I would get the 3am call asking for a lift or an *Uber*. The next day, I'd have to take him to work because his car was already there.

He started saying things like, *"What was I thinking, getting you pregnant? What was I thinking marrying you? I make the money, I can go for a few drinks if I want to. You're not even working, you can't tell me what to do with my money."*

I apologised like any good wife would. He was right. I wasn't working. I was too pregnant and tired and too dramatic with high blood pressure and asshole bosses and being in my last trimester. I was just living off him. I was taking money away from him and his other kids. They cut him off because of me and he was sure to remind me of that whenever he felt necessary.

One day I said to him, *"If you don't want me or the baby, leave now before she gets to know you!"*

I meant it when I said it because I was so upset. He said that the house was his because he was paying it off and I would have to leave, not him, because he was making all the money. He had a point. Even though I had saved the full deposit, by myself while working 16-18-hour days while we were not together, he constantly reminded me that I would have nothing without him.

I decided to stay because I was going to show him that I was going to raise our child right and she was going to love him and I wouldn't be like his ex and turn the kids against him, for *no reason*.

There were so many other red flags that I ignored.

Like the fact that he went out with his work friends and his friend's female cousin ended up spending the night at his place. I was told not to be paranoid. She was just some *"dumb slut"* and he wasn't interested in her because he had me.

As I figured everything out, it was too late. I was way too invested. Plus, I was acting crazy. I was insecure and always jumped the gun and was too sensitive and always yelling at him for no reason. I know this because he told me a lot! Right?

Gaslighting much?

I was doing everything I could to prove to everyone that I was the best wife anyone can ever want. I wasn't going to abandon him like everyone else had. I was going to help him, appreciate him, love him, build him up, encourage him. I was going to be everything that his ex and mother weren't.

He told me that his mother never cooked and all she could do was leave tins and jars of food out for them to eat after school, for e.g. *Spam*, tiny sausages in a jar, tinned beef stew, tinned baked beans, tinned soup etc. I had such a skewed image of them when I met them. He always told me to show his mother how to cook. He always asked me to cook when we visited.

Imagine how self-absorbed I looked, cooking in this woman's kitchen, telling her how I prepare different dishes. I used to only cook stuff at her house that I cooked at home that I knew he liked. I loved to cook so I didn't mind. His mum was always happy to let me use her kitchen.

What is weaponised incompetence?

According to Cleveland Clinic,
"Weaponized incompetence is a psychological dynamic where one person avoids or refuses to do a task and uses their incompetence as an excuse. It can occur in relationships, mostly in committed, romantic relationships."
(Elizabeth Shaw, Overcoming Narcissistic Abuse/ Cleveland Clinic, 2014)

After my surgery, I once asked him to hang out some washing a couple of times. He either threw the entire load into the dryer, or he hung them on coat hangers through the front and back instead of through the shoulders. That would be harder but he managed to do it to every shirt. I had to believe it was intentional. He didn't want to do it.

The clothes ended up stretched, shrunk, wrinkled to oblivion, mouldy because they didn't dry in the over loaded drier. I never said anything. I knew he was waiting for my reaction so we could fight about it and then he'd refuse to help me again.

My ex did nothing around the house. Not even when I had staples and a hole in my head. He was flat out cutting the grass every three to four months. Even then, he carried on about how hard it was. He sulked and complained and expected praise for weeks on end for the one job he did at home. He didn't even do the whole job himself.

As usual, I had to help him with his tasks. He would make my daughter and I go down and collect the toys and clean up after the dog, just so he could walk up and down with minimal effort. He didn't like bending down. He didn't like emptying the catcher. He wanted a bigger lawn mower so he could empty the catcher less often. We argued about this constantly as he already had more tools than he used and still hadn't organised his shed over the five years we had lived there. We had no room. Plus I had to explain to him, the bigger the catcher, the heavier the load.

I even got him a green bin so it would be easier for him to bring the bin to him. Nope, still too hard for him. He just wanted me to go down and do it for him. It was the only job I didn't take on for him. If my back wasn't so broken, I probably would have.

I had no boundaries. I just wanted him to stop complaining.

He would push his plate over to me when he finished eating, like I as a servant waiting to clear the table. He would leave the table as if he were at a restaurant, never helping me clear the table. He would cut bread and leave the crumbs all over the bench. He would complain about the knife he was using and refused to clean up after himself because I didn't have good knives in the kitchen. It was my fault that the knife didn't cut it neatly and made a mess.

An ongoing argument we had was about knives and knife block. He wanted a fancy chucky block. I didn't want a block on the kitchen bench as we didn't have the room. I also hated blocks as they could get mouldy and you would never know because the slots are not visible. He refused to buy knives unless he got to choose the block he wanted. Even though the only thing he ever cut was bread for an easy midnight snack.

He never cooked. Well... he would start sometimes, but it always ended the same way, *"Can you just cut the onions for me, then I'll cook."*

Before I knew it, he was outside having a cigarette, the onions burning on the stove, so of course, I step in and save the meal. Then he doesn't come back to the kitchen until the meal is ready, the table is set and sits down to eat.

I always had to think for him. He was very impulsive and didn't think through the consequences. When he didn't listen to me and his plans ultimately backfired, it was still somehow always my fault. He told me once that I emasculated him.

How can you emasculate someone that doesn't act like a man?

He was and still is a man child.

Then demanded respect... He went to work and made the money. Yes, I'll give him credit for that. But it was hard to be grateful when I knew he was hiding money from me and would literally complain whenever I needed money. This was especially difficult after my surgery. I had no income, and he would complain every time I'd ask him for money.

I know now that this was financial abuse.

He would complain that he had to buy lunch. I explained to him that I can't cook if we don't have groceries at home. He argued that he could afford groceries because he spends so much money on lunches because I don't cook anymore, and don't pack him home made lunches. He had to make me feel like it was my fault.

Everything was my fault. Make it make sense.

He told me one day, *"I usually have a couple of grand sitting in my account, but since your surgery, I got nothing."*

Oh, cry me a river. He was making me feel guilty for having a brain tumour removed. So much for *"in sickness and in health."*

He hated me because I just couldn't physically cope anymore. I owed it to him. I was his wife, the *woman* of the house. I was there to serve him. I owed him everything.

When I was sick with COVID-19, he isolated himself in the room. That way I could still do everything around the house, without making him sick. I was cooking for him, checking if *he* needed anything…

Such a supportive husband, staying out of my way while I felt like I was dying. I was so exhausted, and I needed to rest, but only after I had catered to all his needs.

The more I did, the more he expected. It was never enough.

In our last week together, he kept asking, *"What do you even do for me?"*

Eventually I replied, *"Nothing! Is that what you want to hear?"*

He was slightly shocked and then replied, *"About time you admit it."*

Fuck you!

I laughed. I had enough of his abuse and accusations. I had no energy to fight. No energy to defend myself, to explain again what I do for this man. He didn't appreciate anything for 17 years. He wasn't suddenly going to understand it.

I was laying down one day, trying to rest. He came in and said, *"Oh you're laying down again? What's for dinner? You're on Facebook all day, that's why you're tired. That's why you have a headache."*

I'm sure it had nothing to do with my surgery.

How dare I be laying down when he was at work all day? I had already cleaned the whole house, done a few loads of laundry, cooked dinner and had a doctor's appointment, but when he saw me laying down, I hadn't done anything all day. He hated me being on my phone for any reason. Even when I was running the business.

GOOD LITTLE GREEK GIRL

He never respected my time. I belonged to him and my time was only for him. He used to call me to pick him up from work. Our daughter was only about six months old. He would call and tell me when to leave the house. I would sit in the car with the baby for up to three hours, waiting for him to actually finish. He kept saying, *"Yeah, coming now."*

The baby would get so uncomfortable and hungry and wet. He didn't like when the baby fussed when he was in the car. It was when he started to complain I spoke up about the ridiculously long waiting times. I asked him to call when he was actually finished, not when he thought they might be finishing soon. He refused.

He would rather have the baby, and I sit and wait for him for literal hours, rather than him wait 10 minutes for us to come from home. Incredibly selfish, however, he always knew how to twist the narrative so that I would feel unreasonable for making him wait when he's been at work all day and he was so tired, and I was doing nothing at home all day.

Chapter 13

Discovering and Embodying My Life Path

GOOD LITTLE GREEK GIRL

They say that earth angels have an agreement with God/higher power that we will *serve* while on earth. We each need to work out what we are meant for. We have all forgotten what our true path is and we have to work on rediscovering that.

I am a healer. I have a photo of me, no older than two years old, sitting on a complete strangers lap.

The gentleman was sitting alone on the grass. My mother recalls that he seemed very sad and lonely. I took it upon myself to approach this man and show him some kindness and love. The man is smiling ear to ear in the photo. I'd have to agree that it worked.

I speak the truth. I used to hide but it was always so much harder and more stressful to tell lies, even if they were to avoid conflict, even if they were safer than the truth.

One day, I simply decided I would just speak the truth and I can't explain how freeing it was.

I never lied again. Throat chakra unblocked.

This went against everything I had ever known. I knew to shut up and hide so no one got upset. I watched adults lie all the time, knowing that it was necessary to keep the peace, but who's peace was it keeping?

Scream therapy might be exactly what I need right now. I'm finally allowing myself to see a different perspective of my life – especially when it comes to apologising and acknowledging my own wrongs. I've developed a habit of taking the blame, of constantly seeing myself as the one at fault, and that's deeply rooted in how I was raised, in the environments and groups I was part of. My mistakes were always highlighted, always under a spotlight.

But now that I'm healing, it's so important that I start putting the blame where it actually belongs. And I want to explain why.

When I was in survival mode, I became so comfortable with the mask I had to wear just to get through the day – to feel normal, to fit into society – that when I finally woke up and admitted I never liked the life I claimed as mine, people were surprised. They couldn't understand how I could play the game so well and then just reject it. They saw me as a liar. And I started gaslighting myself, too – thinking maybe I really was lying.

I told myself, *"I must have liked it, right? I said I did. I tried so hard to make it work."*

But survival mode literally creates new neural pathways – illusions – that veil me from my truth. Because if I had accepted the truth back then, I would've had to face how unsafe, how dangerous, my environment really was. And that felt impossible. I had to survive long enough to escape.

It's a paradox: I knew deep down I wasn't supposed to be in that life, but I had to stay in it just to get out. So I veiled myself, numbed myself, made myself believe I needed that life to survive. But at the same time, I was secretly working on an escape plan.

GOOD LITTLE GREEK GIRL

It's like living a double life – undercover in my own existence. Pretending to belong, to be part of a world I was plotting to leave. And somewhere along the way, I forgot I was even undercover. I was so deep in the mission that I started to believe the role I was playing. I became the mask.

But now I'm waking up. I'm starting to remember who I really am. I stayed undercover for so long, I started building my entire reality around that false identity. My neural pathways were shaped by it.

And I don't owe anyone an apology for that.

I don't owe people apologies for the ways I showed up while I was in survival mode. I don't owe them an apology for lying to them – because I lied to them the same way I lied to myself. I had to. To stay alive.

They never apologised to me for creating an environment where I had to hide. So before I ever think about apologising to them, I need to apologise to *myself* – for feeling guilty about doing what I had to do to survive.

What a beautiful heart I must have, to feel shame for the lies I told to stay alive, when they never took accountability for making me feel like I had no choice but to lie in the first place.

It was too hard to explain the reality I was in. The deception around me came and went so quickly – just flashes of truth that disappeared as fast as they appeared. I was left wondering if I ever saw it at all.

DISCOVERING AND EMBODYING MY LIFE PATH

I did not know you Sir, but I had love for you.

GOOD LITTLE GREEK GIRL

And eventually, I convinced myself I was crazy. I made myself believe I was imagining the monsters that flickered in and out of my reality. But I wasn't. The people around me were cloaked in lies for so long, I began to question my own intuition. My truth felt like a lie because it came in such brief, painful glimpses – and then disappeared again.

So, I gave in to the lie. I accepted the story they wrote for me, the mask they expected me to wear. I lied to myself the same way they lied to themselves. I lied to them the same way they lied to the world.

It was all a veil. And I was just trying to survive.

There were moments I saw the truth – brief, terrifying flashes of it – and I would ask myself, *"Did that really happen?"*

But the cloak would fall back into place, and the confusion would return.

So now, I'm turning the apology around. I'm releasing the shame I've held in my heart for lying about who I really was. I didn't lie to hurt anyone. I lied to protect myself. I lied because telling the truth back then would've meant the end of me.

Before I apologise to the world, I'm apologising to myself – for hiding my needs, for convincing myself that the environment I adapted to was ever meant to be my home.

<u>I forgive myself.</u>

DISCOVERING AND EMBODYING MY LIFE PATH

I grieve for the small life I accepted, the limited version of myself I clung to because I was too afraid to be seen.

Now, as my world expands, as my authenticity blooms, I reintroduce myself to the world – and I know some people will call me a liar. They only ever knew the mask. They're limited by their own view of me.

And that's okay. I'll smile in my truth. I'll keep speaking it, even if it feels like a lie at first – because I wore the cloak so long that my truth has to be relearned.

My old 'truth' is crumbling. And in its place, the real me is emerging.

I'm letting myself grieve.

Grieve the lies I lived.

Grieve the truths I ran from.

I'm showing myself grace as I learn who I am now – free from the fear that being seen means being destroyed.

I am letting myself be seen.

Letting myself be uncovered.

Letting myself be discovered.

And those who always saw my truth? They'll stand by me – not saying, *"I knew it,"* but simply standing there, holding space. Because they know how painful it is to realise that your entire life was a lie.

They've been there, too.

So I let go.
I surrender.
And I let the truth – *my* truth – shine.

Let them gawk.

Let them wonder.

Because they'll never get to experience the fullness of who I really am. That's a privilege reserved for those who truly *see* me.

I was stuck on 'better the devil you know'.

That soon became, *"Fuck the devil, I don't want one in my life."*

Chapter 14

Quotes That Felt Personal

GOOD LITTLE GREEK GIRL

*"'Cause I'm too messy, and then I'm too fucking clean
You told me get a job, then you ask where the hell I've been
And I'm too perfect till I open my big mouth
I want to be me, is that not allowed?
And I'm too clever, and then I'm too fucking dumb
You hate it when I cry unless it's that time of the month
And I'm too perfect till I show you that I'm not
A thousand people I could be for you, and you hate the fucking lot."*
(Lola Young, 'Messy', 2024)

"What you're not changing, you're choosing."
(Laurie Buchanan)

"Having a high pain tolerance, is just an understanding of pain. When you recognise what 100% is, then you find comfort in knowing it can't get worse. I can adjust to the pain, knowing that if I adjust then there is nothing beyond that."
(Ben Cole-Edwards)

"If you feel an overwhelming sense of sadness after spending time with family, it's not because you don't love them. It's because being around them makes you revert back to an old version of yourself, one you've outgrown. Your brain associates family with outdated roles, past wounds and suppressed emotions, making it difficult to feel like the person you've worked so hard to become."
(Mathew Mortarana)

QUOTES THAT FELT PERSONAL

"Narcissists will use something called Forced Teaming to make you do the things they want you to do or want you to do for them. It creates a synthetic owed loyalty from your end to them. They do this is a subtle way. They merge histories, experiences, backgrounds and especially traumas, so you start to feel it back to back, you and them against the world. It seems innocent at the beginning, but they'll pull on it for leverage. It's another tactic to control you. If this doesn't work, they'll use fear, obligation, guilt, essentially inducing shame in you so that you comply... A narcissist will minimise any contribution, sacrifice or value you hold to ground zero, while magnifying their own slightest inconveniences to a hundredfold to what it actually is. And again, this is a more desperate measure in order to force your compliance... Don't try to prove anything to them... They cannot live in reality because they have broken reality testing. It will only get worse and lead to you being more invalidated. You need to cut them out. You need to Reality Test with people who are healthy and don't live in perpetual delusion."
(Daniel James aka Shadow DeAngelis, 2025)

"Growing up with Emotionally Immature Parents, means you're the adult when it benefits them, but the second you say no, you're treated like a clueless kid. That kind of emotional whiplash screws with your sense of reality and leaves you constantly second guessing yourself. Parenting your Emotionally Immature Parents isn't working because they are stuck in their own past traumas."
(Carolyn Michele Middlesdorf, 2025)

"Trauma is not a memory, It is reliving... You are not remembering what happened yesterday, you are reliving what happened yesterday. You feel like it's happening right now, that's the nature of trauma. You relive sensory details, what can you smell, what can you hear? The timekeeper of your brain switches off."
(Bassel Van Der Kolk, 2025)

2. "Fierce Independence: Your 'I don't need anyone' attitude might be a shield. It can come from learning early on that you can't rely on others.
2. Constant People-Pleasing: This isn't just 'being nice'. It can be a learned survival tactic to earn love and avoid rejection.
3. Hating Stillness: Always have to be busy? This can be a way to outrun the anxiety that surfaces when you're alone with your thoughts.
4. Serial Monogamy: Jumping from one relationship to the next isn't always about romance. It can be driven by a deep fear of being alone.
5. Difficulty with Small Talk: Hating surface-level chats can be about more than introversion. It's a way to dodge the vulnerability that real connection requires.
6. Oversharing Too Soon: 'Trauma dumping' on a first date? This can be a frantic attempt to fast-track intimacy out of a fear they'll leave.
7. Being a 'Fixer': Always drawn to partners you can 'save'? This may stem from a childhood where you had to be a caretaker to feel worthy of love.
8. Extreme Rejection Sensitivity: An intense reaction to a minor slight can signal a deep-rooted and painful fear of abandonment.

9. Crippling Perfectionism: This isn't just high standards. It's often a belief that you must be flawless to be loved and accepted.

10. Scorekeeping in Relationships: Meticulously tracking who did what? This points to a fundamental lack of trust and fear of being exploited.

11. Shutting Down in Conflict: Immediately withdrawing during an argument is a defence mechanism. It's a sign that emotions feel overwhelming and unsafe.

12. The Push-Pull Dynamic: Craving intimacy, then feeling suffocated when it happens? This is a classic sign of wanting connection but also being terrified of it.

13. Idealizing New Partners: Falling hard and fast while ignoring red flags can be driven by a deep longing for the security you never had.

14. Not Knowing Your Needs: If you genuinely don't know what you want or need, you may have learned to suppress your needs after they were consistently ignored.

15. Feeling Chronically Empty: This isn't just a mood. It can mean you learned to disconnect from your feelings long ago just to cope."

(Mathew Martorana, 2025)

Chapter 15

Nothing Changes, If Nothing Changes!

GOOD LITTLE GREEK GIRL

I'm sitting here, listening to my parents argue, again.

It's a beautiful Sunday, so naturally we're spring cleaning.

My dad has been vacuuming for about an hour and the entire time, he has been cursing the floor, the furniture, the rugs, the vacuum. My mum is hovering as she does best, exacerbating the chaos that is usually a very boring, uneventful, unemotional job.

I feel like I should break up the fight again but then I remember, I'm not here to parent my parents. They fight all day every day. They deny it but can't start a conversation without it leading to angry words. Their interaction literally is comment, reply, fight. I'm exhausted by it. Their energy drains me and makes me miserable. I hate that I let it affect me so much.

I studied shadow work, embodiment, transmuting the negative to positives.,understanding my triggers. I had some serious shadow work to do, and I had to learn to embody my authentic self. Every day, I realise I still have so much work to do. Yes, I have come a long way, but in hindsight it's the first three steps on the Great Wall of China.

Every word that comes out of my mother's mouth is either, accusatory, judgmental, mean, condescending. But she doesn't see it. She tells me it in my head and I choose to be offended by everything she says. I don't get offended anymore, but I sure as hell point it out because she still has a huge influence on my eight-year-old daughter. She can be kind. She can be the best, but we see less and less of that.

NOTHING CHANGES, IF NOTHING CHANGES!

My father is almost 70yrs old. You wouldn't believe the tantrums this man throws on the daily. My daughter talks about emotional intelligence, yeah, the 8,yr old. She tells him how to get back to the *green zone*. How to *breathe*.

I left my marriage to remove my daughter from a toxic environment, and every day I fear that coming to live with my parents is equally detrimental. It comes down to options and money. I made the best choice I could from the options I had.

I see my dad as a small, deeply wounded child that was given a strong man's body.

I know how he grew up and the abuse he endured. His father was an asshole until the day he died. He tormented my dad even after death by showing his unwavering favouritism to my dad's younger brother.

He loves my brother and I and gives us everything we need, financially. He tries his best to provide emotional support, but it may be too little too late, but I appreciate and accept the effort. His demons still surface and he still has violent outbursts but it's better than it was. He is softer than he used to be.. *Or* am I just so conditioned that I see silver lining where it doesn't exist. Is he more loving or has he just mastered manipulation. Is he better at playing the victim?

Chapter 16

Goosfraba

GOOD LITTLE GREEK GIRL

If you've ever seen the Adam Sandler movie, *'Anger Management'*, then you might remember the *'Goosfraba'* scene. In the movie, it is used as a mantra to calm down, like counting to 10 when you are angry.

"Goosfraba" is not an English word. Goosfraba is actually a word that Eskimos use to calm their children down. Some people hum *"Om"* to calm their anger, but Goosfraba has really stuck with me.

Did you know that the Inuit people never scald their children? The children do not misbehave and never have screaming tantrums. They don't do it because they are never given this example of dealing with their emotions. Monkey see monkey do?

Imagine that everyone around you had a calm way of dealing with stress. Imagine that if the example was a deep breath, sitting silent and focusing on mantras to calm yourself. Imagine if that is all you knew. Total bliss if you ask me.

Now compare this to the examples you actually had. I know it was and still is the complete opposite to that.

I grew up with the example being that: You yelled, you cried and mixed in guilt and a version of what's to come, always being the worst-case scenario, you made sure you let everyone see you stamp your feet and slam doors and use disrespectful or threatening language then follow up with the silent treatment for days instead of apologising and talking it through.

If you were angry enough, you broke something. If you were too emotional, you didn't talk about it, you drank or smoked or used illicit drugs. Or you formed a gambling habit. If you were a real man, you would make sure your family feared you. Fear equals respect, right? You had every right to lay hands on another person or at least scream so loud your body shivered and your face was so close to theirs that your breath mixed with the tears on their face.

Terrible behaviour that doesn't fly in the real world, right? So, we learn to become inauthentic and outcome the masks, we learnt to adapt when we were children, now as adults struggling with what is ingrained in us and what the outside world expects from us.

My initial reaction is to be loud and obvious in my reactions. I learnt that I had to be aggressive, just to be heard. Or at least feel like I tried my hardest to be.

Just because this is what we saw, this is not what was acceptable. Mirroring your parents' behaviour always got you in trouble. Why is that? Because they saw how loud, disruptive, disrespectful, and utterly pointless a reaction like that really is. Sadly, they never took accountability for their behaviour. They never tried to improve. And they still scald me for my behaviour. I am still waiting for them to show me how.

My daughter and I had to move back in with my parents after I separated from my second husband. I tell you nothing has changed since I was a kid. I still have to de-escalate arguments.

I am still fighting to be heard. I am still trying to set boundaries. I am still trying to make them see how their words affect others.

I fight every day so that they do not impact my daughter the same way they did me. I am not saying they *have* to change, but they really should not be surprised that they are being cut off from family and social groups because of how they interact.

The relationship I have with my daughter is very different. Firstly, I speak to her with respect, and I demonstrate kindness and understanding. I show her how respect is earnt and not scared into you by force. I encourage her to talk to me about anything and everything and I validate her feelings and opinions.

Please do not take me wrong here. It sounds like I am still blaming them for my bad behaviour. I do not anymore. I know that I am responsible for my own actions and how I deal with my own triggers.

My dream is to open a one stop shop for healing, wellbeing and finding peace. I might even call it, *'Goosfraba: Normalising Support for One Another'*. I'll have to work out how to write that!

It will literally be a one stop shop for counselling, meditation, somatic yoga, smash rage room, scream (soundproof) room, laughing room, psychiatry, naturopath, nutritionist, crystal healing, detoxing, lymphatic drainage, massage. I also am very passionate about providing domestic violence support, emergency accommodation.

A dignity station, a free shower and laundry, free haircuts and lice treatments, free clothes, help with resumes and job interviews. I would love to partner with others, like *Orange Sky* and *The Good Box*. I would love to visit schools and let the children know that there is help available if they are seeing any kind of abuse at home. The help can be for them or a friend or family member.

Chapter 17

The Cut Off Game

GOOD LITTLE GREEK GIRL

My cut off game is so strong. I no longer tolerate any disrespect. Since my separation form my husband, I dated a guy for four months and I broke up with him because his communication was lacking. He was extremely busy. But no one is too busy to text a simple good morning, have a good day, or good night. So simple yet so hard for some.

I expressed my feelings so many times about being ignored for days at a time. I got an apology the first time, then the excuses started, then the resentment. You don't get to be made at me for expecting the bare minimum, goodbye now.

But why can't I cut off my parents? They have crossed all my boundaries more than anyone I've ever met.

The most obvious answer is survival. I'm in a position now where I need them to provide a roof over my daughter's head. I'm just here as part of that package. The way my marriage ended, I had nowhere else to go. My husband refused to leave the house. He made me leave with my daughter.

According to my ex, it was too hard for a single guy on $140k a year to find a place to rent. It's much easier for a single mother, that can't work due to medical issues.

I wasn't exactly welcome here. I still don't know if I am. I still feel like a burden. I had to spell it out to my parents, *"Come and pick us up or my daughter and I are going to a woman's shelter tonight!"*

Do you know what it feels like to beg for support from your parents?

I guess part of me is here out of spite. They will help me now because this is their fault!

They didn't speak up when I was asking for help with my husband. They didn't want to get involved but would complain to me about his behaviour.

Hello! I'm the one living it. You're just a spectator.

I know exactly what is happening. They didn't teach me how to advocate for or support myself. I ended up in this relationship because of the examples I grew up with. I knew only to shut up and put up. How to keep trying to seek approval and appreciation. How to sacrifice in order to stay married, no matter the quality of the union.

I do love my parents, and they will love me, too. Even if I have to force them to.

I'm not sounding very sane right now. But it is what it is.

Is this cruel of me? No. because I know I love them and I know I'm going to be here to take care of them as they age. I won't abandon them. We fight all the time but I see effort and growth on their end.

You should never expect anyone to change. You will die waiting, however you can encourage others to grow, for themselves, not for anyone else.

Let me clarify at this moment, forgiveness is not what's going to heal me.

GOOD LITTLE GREEK GIRL

What will heal me is acknowledging, validating, and learning to truly feel through my pain. I have to see just how much my parents' unconscious actions affected me – how they left deep emotional wounds inside of me.

I'm learning to allow myself to feel the anger, the sadness, the fear – all the emotions that are a natural response to abuse, neglect, or simply not having my needs met.

And when I do this in the right way – through my connection to my body, my nervous system, and my subconscious – I begin to release the pain. I start to feel peace. What fills that space is love and forgiveness, even for the people who hurt me – including my parents.

I can't skip to forgiveness if I haven't truly processed the pain.

If I cut them off. No goodbye. No conversation. Just straight silence.

They won't get to see their grandchild. They won't know what they did, and they'll never get the chance to make it right. I remember one of them saying, *"I raised you the best I could, and now you say I'm toxic. I don't even know what that means."*

And the other one said, *"I'm still your mum. Doesn't that count for something?"*

They're carrying decades of pain and shame they didn't even know they still held. And now it's turning into rage, sadness, confusion.

THE CUT OFF GAME

We live in a world that teaches us to cut people off and protect our own peace. But I'm starting to see that peace without healing isn't actually peace. It's avoidance wrapped in a pretty coat.

This isn't about blaming myself or them. It's about naming the wound. Acknowledging the harm. Accepting the impact from both sides – me as the child, them as the parents. And then asking: What if we could repair without erasing everything? What if I could set boundaries and still build bridges?

Because no one wins in a broken lineage. And deep down, I don't want that disconnection.

If I'm the child who walks away – I'll have my reasons. But there's always going to be a voice in my heart that wonders what could've been.

I don't want to cut them off.

Healing isn't going to start by waiting. It starts by choosing to understand. By choosing to listen. By choosing to love bigger than my pain.

Waiting on a understanding that might never come.

Some say Hollywood made propaganda that quietly tore apart the family unit. Every show I grew up watching told the same story: Parents are stupid, toxic, disposable. They don't care. Stay distant. Cut them out. Friends matter more than family. Even the kids' shows followed that formula.

Repeatedly we saw mums who belittled their kids, dads who were lazy, aggressive, or absent. Rarely did I ever see a story about repairing a family or working through conflict.

Maybe they used it because they knew relatable story lines would make for better ratings.

My whole generation believes that cutting off your parents is just part of being an adult. That distance is freedom. That found family is always better than real family. Cutting people off is praised. Avoidance is called healing.

As long as we are honest and accountable for our own behaviour and we remember it's not about pointing the finger and being a victim, I think it is healthy that we are doing so. Any video I've watched about healing a toxic relationship with your parents, always state, *"Except in the occasion of abuse."*

No two stories or situations are the same. We all need to know our *why* and then sort out our own *how*.

I grew up in a house where no one ever said sorry. Where silence meant anger.

I've realised I learned to over-share, over-text, over-explain – because I can't breathe until the air is cleared. I beg for forgiveness. I push for resolution because childhood chaos taught me to fix everything instantly, or just pretend it never happened.

When someone shuts down, I feel like I've done something wrong. I'm in trouble. That hits me like a punch in the gut.

THE CUT OFF GAME

My stomach knots, my chest tightens, my mind spins and overthinks. It's the same old movie on repeat.

But here's the truth: It's not the fight that hurts me most – it's my nervous system replaying my deepest childhood fear: *"If no one apologises, I'm forgotten, I'm not worth it, they hate me. I don't matter."*

Now I'm ready to break that loop.

I remind myself that safety lives inside me. Not in someone's response. Not in their validation. Not in the fixing or the reply. Just in me.

And I do this again and again, every conflict, every moment and I start to watch the anxiety drop and the connection rise. Because that tension I feel is not about the moment.

It's my inner child, begging for peace.

GOOD LITTLE GREEK GIRL

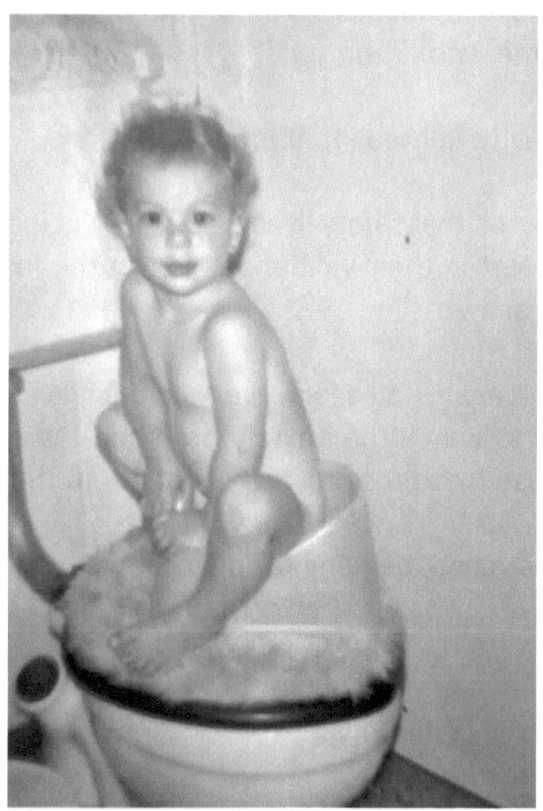

I have always had my own way of doing things.

Chapter 18

Understanding Beyond the Physical

GOOD LITTLE GREEK GIRL

"You will absorb every single thought that your mother thinks and that she feels is a vibration that you will absorb.

- Not good enough.
- I have to be perfect to be loved.
- It's selfish to put myself first.
- Money is hard to get.
- Emotion is weakness.
- Failure is not an option.

It's not only the way that your father treated you, but your mother also treated you. It's not only the way that they raised you, but it's the vibration within the household.

- I can't ask for help.
- Resting means I'm lazy.
- Life is not fair.
- I'm too much
- Love has to be earned.
- People won't like the Real Me.

Now, when you're able to identify all of the limiting beliefs that not only your family has but also that you have inherited you are able to grab on to them and heal them so that you don't give these to your children, and then you keep this cycle, rolling in the generational trauma."

(Loveagainjen, TikTok, 2025)

UNDERSTANDING BEYOND THE PHYSICAL

Jen, the author of *The Shadow Within*, explains how our behaviour is shaped. She explains that these aren't beliefs; They are vibrations that you absorb. Parents' vibrated within these fears and children absorb energy like a sponge. This means that everything you believe and holds you back, was given from someone else. Not you.

You were born pure, with no fears, and with the belief that you can achieve anything. This is taken away from you and only YOU can choose to clean... and take it back.

When I was completing my Diploma of Social Sciences and Social Work, I learnt about Maslow's Hierarchy of Needs, Sigmund Fraud's theories about oppressing emotions and unconscious memories in early childhood. Freud abandoned the theory that every neurosis can be traced back to the effects of abuse, they became pathogenic only when acting as repressed memory. We learnt about how children are super receptive and collect data that adults don't even know they're putting out there.

It would be another 25 years before I understood that on a whole new level. A level of Shadow Work and owning my personal triggers.

I remember discussing my perspective with my teacher, Ross. I explained to him that two children growing up in the same house, with the same parents, can be taught two very different standards, morals and beliefs.

I was speaking from experience as I was speaking about my brother and I. Although my brother received harsher physical abuse from our father, they made it up to him when he was older.

My abuse was definitely more emotional and psychological. I also got hit. I would run to my room and throw my body weight behind the door to keep my dad away from me. That would give him time to calm down. His temper has always been a huge problem, even today and he is in his late 60s.

I remember one time, my brother had covered his ears to block out Dad yelling at him. My dad slapped him, like someone smashing large cymbals together, with my brother's head in between the palms of his hands. My brother was being *"disrespectful",* by covering his ears. How else would my parents deal with that? Obviously no talking involved. Yelling, but no talking.

During altercations we heard, *"I'm going to step on your throat. I'm going to hit you so hard, you'll forget where you came from. I'm going to murder you. I'm going to smash your body into pieces. I'll give you something to cry about."*

We never heard, *"Can you tell me what's wrong? Can you tell me what happened? Come take a deep breath and sit down. Why are you covering your ears?"*

We usually got hit on the backside or on the legs. My dad would grab my face and squeeze. His palm under my chin, his thumb on one side and his other fingers on the other. Stopping my mouth and jaw from moving, but I would still squeal.

UNDERSTANDING BEYOND THE PHYSICAL

He slapped me around the mouth area to teach me not to say disrespectful words. He would only hit with his pointer and middle finger, but it still hurt.

It was still scary as hell and was a direct reminder of his dominance and power.

Chapter 19

The Way the Cycle Repeats Itself

GOOD LITTLE GREEK GIRL

I was at the dinner table the other night at my parents' house. Dad was drinking again.

We were talking about something simple, but in three seconds flat, it turned into another nasty fight. Dad's hands in my face again. My mother was trying to control the narrative *again*.

Today, my mother told me to just let him have his tantrum and be quiet and let it blow over. I told her, *"I will not submit to his abuse anymore. Next time he puts his fingers in my face, I'll snap the fucking things off."*

I'm so sick of the constant abuse. I'm sick of walking on eggshells. I'm sick of forcing myself to be invisible. Just before this conversation, she was telling me about how he exerts financial abuse. He has done this their entire marriage.

She wants a divorce, but I told her I'm not here to take care of him. He needs professional help. If she leaves, she better deal with him like everyone else has to deal with ex-husbands.

She will not pass on anymore of this fuckery to me.

My mother tried to threaten me by saying I'd end up hurt if I didn't back down and I responded, "Well he might just end up in jail then."

I'm so done with bullies. I'm exhausted and have no tolerance for any of it anymore.

THE WAY THE CYCLE REPEATS ITSELF

It shows me her mindset is still stuck in the 30s. The victim is to blame. It makes me want to cry.

It also shows again how some people will not come with you. Some people will just stay exactly where and how they are.

I heard one that we can only help people so much before we start to interfere with their karma and their life path. If we interfere too much, they miss the lesson they were meant to learn and they end up having to relive the difficulty that was supposed to teach them something.

We should understand that for ourselves as well. We need to face our own narrative and learn from it.

We have to know that everything does happen for a reason.

Every hardship is a lesson.

A pathway to our true self, that we have forgotten to be.

Chapter 20

Speak Up

GOOD LITTLE GREEK GIRL

When I was a child, I was part of a study for the *Mater Hospital*. University students would come to my home, and I'd fill out a questionnaire and then have a one-on-one interview. I knew then, by the questions on the form, that domestic abuse was something that happened to a lot of people, but it was still something no one was comfortable talking about. I didn't know if I had found allies or just more people I had to play dumb with.

I watched the students choke on the questions and rush me through my answers. They were not allies. They didn't really want to know how it affected me. They just wanted to get some ticks on the form and leave. No one was going to look at these answers. They were just going to count up the ticks in the column and become a statistic on someone's report that not many people would read.

No one was coming to help.

It was just another half-ass attempt of someone coming to do a job with no real change, even though they were handed information of children in need of help.

I didn't hear anything about domestic abuse until I was in my late 30s. It just was never spoken about. By some miracle, I was introduced to a group of women through a friend. We met once a week via *Zoom* with a life coach.

For the first time in my life, someone wanted to *hear* me and they wanted to *support* me. I spoke without fear of judgment or resentment. Without being cut off. With out having my words twisted.

For the first time ever, someone told me that it wasn't all in my head. I wasn't crazy. I was enough. I was a victim of domestic violence, and it was not okay. They told me I wasn't the problem.

Until this point, I thought I was the problem. *Everything* was my fault. I just wasn't doing enough. I wasn't patient enough. Wasn't fit enough. I was too cranky. Too emotional.

I finally allowed myself to understand my reactions to other people's treatment. It wasn't because I was unreasonable. It was because I was getting upset by the lack of appreciation and respect.

My life started changing. I started standing up for myself. I was finally giving my emotions a voice. I tried to explain myself, hoping that maybe if my ex understood how he hurt me he would stop. That didn't go well.

It didn't take me long to realise I was wasting my breath. He didn't care. It just angered him that I was pointing things out.

Eventually, I was unbothered. I had given up. That's when he got nastier, trying to scare me into staying. Making me feel powerless, invisible, hopeless, useless.

The day I left, he said, *"I don't know what else to do. I begged, I threatened I've tried everything."*

I replied, *"All I wanted from you was kindness and love."*

That was obviously too much to ask for.

Finally, conversations about narcissistic abuse, physical, emotional, financial abuse are becoming more mainstream. People are sharing their experiences. People are realising that they are not alone. They are recognising the signs. They are empowering themselves.

30 odd years later, the world is changing.

The smallest changes can make a huge impact. We just need to keep speaking up.

Don't be scared to be the odd one out.

Say what everyone else is thinking but no one is saying.

Be the voice for those who don't have one yet.

Chapter 21

Dear Mum

GOOD LITTLE GREEK GIRL

Dear Mum,

I love you.

I'm sorry that you have had such a hard life. I know you were such a sweet, innocent child that wouldn't hurt a fly. I'm sorry that Yiayia and Pappou were so strict and that your brothers were assholes to you, too.

I'm sorry that you didn't get to date dad before you got to marry him. I'm sorry you were forced to rush the marriage and you didn't get to know him well enough.

I'm sorry you were taken out of school in eighth grade so you could work in the sewing factory. You are so smart, and I think if you were given the opportunity, you could have become something high ranking, like a judge, a surgeon, or a university lecturer.

Your empathy is your greatest quality, and your greatest weakness. You have had your empathy and kindness used against you. It hasn't been appreciated.

You always prioritised everyone else's needs over your own.

Please stop scalding me for being 'controversial'. I cannot support injustice, no matter the consequences for myself.

Do you remember the Monkey Experiment? Google the *Monkeys, Bananas and Ladder Experiment* (2025). Moral of the story: Rules and norms can persist beyond their logical or practical relevance, simply because they have been established and maintained over time. This demonstrates the tendency of individuals and groups to adhere to traditions and practices that may no longer make sense.

I wish you had more time to discipline my brother and teach him how to act like a caring big brother, instead of an entitled prick, that found joy in tormenting me. I've tried so hard not to hate him.

I wish that when you moved to Australia, you lived with other cultures and got to see how the rest of the world worked. You all moved to West End with every other Greek and the village mentality stayed with you all.

Your family was so scared of losing its identity that you resisted change and you doubled down on the rules, traditions, morals, that you lived in your little, secluded village. You had a chance for a fresh start.

Unfortunately, that wasn't the case, and the Greeks that stayed behind in Greece evolved and the Greeks that Immigrated all stayed stuck in the old ways.

I wish that what happened to your Yiayia would have taught you all not to give so much power to others' opinions and gossip. Your family should have stood up for her. They knew she was a good woman. But for some reason, she felt so alone that she didn't think anyone would disagree with the priest. Why didn't anyone have her back? Family is supposed to support each other.

GOOD LITTLE GREEK GIRL

Instead, everyone probably told her to hurry up and make everything right, when I wish she had someone telling her, *"Don't worry about anyone else. You have a big, beautiful family and a new baby and a man that loves you. No two life paths are the same. Let them talk."*

She just needed her family on her side. She needed someone to stand by her and tell her she was a good woman. Someone to stand by her side and face the wrath with her.

That's all I've ever wanted from you and Dad. Just back me up. Believe in me.

> *"The ultimate measure of a man is not where he stands in moments of comfort and convenience, but where he stands at times of challenge and controversy."*
> (Martin Luther King Jr.)

Chapter 22

Dear Dad

GOOD LITTLE GREEK GIRL

Dear Dad,

I love you.

I'm sorry that you had such a horrible, unfair childhood.

I'm sorry that your parents never showed you real, unconditional love.

I'm sorry they were too stupid to appreciate you and I'm sorry they were too jealous to be proud of you.

I'm sorry that your baby brothers were favoured for no particular reason.

I wish you could see in yourself that you are one of the strongest men I know. You can be very supportive. Loving. But you don't love yourself. I wish that you could see that you deserve a life that isn't punishment. I wish you would appreciate what you have and had a different attitude toward life.

Thank you for working so hard to give us a financially secure future. Would it be so bad if you enjoyed some of it now?

I wish you understood that respect is earnt in love, not forced by fear. Being kind is not a weakness. I'm glad to see you have softened over the years.

Softened is not a criticism, it's a compliment.

DEAR DAD

You have always been such a mean control freak. You were never fair to Mum. You should worship the ground that she walks on. You have been a horrible *partner*. The only support you have provided is financial. Which is great, but money hasn't bought you a happy union. I wish you could see how your narcissistic traits have destroyed her.

I see your misery but can't sympathise because I see that it's self-inflicted.

No one hates you more than you hate yourself.

You are responsible to heal yourself. And one day, I hope that you do.

Chapter 23

It's Not the End

GOOD LITTLE GREEK GIRL

They say time heals all wounds and although it has taken me some time to work through everything that I needed to do to find myself and begin again.

I'm excited for what lays ahead knowing that I have everything within me to face any obstacle that might try to derail me in the future.

For anyone that this book might have inspired, I hope that it helps you find your true north and live your best life.

With love,
Dama

Resources

GOOD LITTLE GREEK GIRL

A few friends you never knew you had:

QLD
1800 RESPECT	1800 7377328
CENTRE CARE	3251 5000
WOMENS HEALTH AND EQUALITY QUEENSLAND	3216 0376
RELATIONSHIPS AUSTRALIA	1300 364 277
VICTIMCONNECT	1300 318 940
BRISBANE DOMESTIC VIOLENCE SERVICES	3217 2544
ZIG ZAG, YOUNG WOMANS RECOURCE CENTRE	3843 1823
BRISBANE RAPE INCEST SURVIVORS	3391 0004
IMMAGRANT WOMENS SUPPORT	3846 3490
*(Call TIS National on **131 450**)*	
WWILD SEXUAL VIOLENCEE PROGRAM	3262 9877
WOMENS HEALTH AND EQUITY	3216 0376
DV CONNECT MENS LINE	1800 600 636
MENSLINE AUSTRALIA	1300 789 978

Other states:
- *Family violence statewide support services | vic.gov.au*
- *Family and domestic violence helplines and support services SA.GOV.AU*
- *Domestic and family violence and sexual assault support services*
- *Domestic, family and sexual violence | NT.GOV.AU*
- *Domestic and family violence support | NSW Government Family Violence Support Services, Tasmania Police*
- *Reach out to your local police service or healthcare professionals to get you in touch with the right service.*

About the Author

GOOD LITTLE GREEK GIRL

Born in Queensland in 1982 to Greek immigrant parents, Eleni grew up in a world marked by silence, sacrifice, and the shadows of domestic violence and narcissistic abuse. Yet from that pain, she found the seeds of resilience — especially since becoming a mother and refusing to let her daughter repeat history.

Over the past two decades, she has dedicated herself to both personal and professional growth, working in community and customer services, studying breath-work, shadow work, and art therapy, as well as learning from many respected mentors.

Her own healing journey has become the foundation of her purpose: to uplift and inspire others who are walking through their own struggles. Through her writing, Eleni shares her story with honesty and compassion, offering hope, courage, and a powerful reminder that while the path to healing is deeply personal, it is never one we walk alone.

www.ingramcontent.com/pod-product-compliance
Lightning Source LLC
Chambersburg PA
CBHW020416080526
44584CB00014B/1360